Ane Maria Gammo
12/24/97
Ames, Iowa

African-American
Reflections on Brazil's
Racial Paradise

African-American Reflections on Brazil's Racial Paradise

Edited by *David J. Hellwig*

Temple University Press
Philadelphia

Temple University Press, Philadelphia 19122
Copyright © 1992 by Temple University. All rights reserved
Published 1992
Printed in the United States of America

The paper used in this publication meets the minimum requirements of
American National Standard for Information Sciences—Permanence of Paper
for Printed Library Materials, ANSI Z39.48-1984

Library of Congress Cataloging-in-Publication Data
African-American reflections on Brazil's racial paradise / edited by David J.
Hellwig.
   p. cm.
  Includes bibliographical references.
  ISBN 0-87722-892-2 :
  1. Blacks—Brazil—History. 2. Brazil—Race relations—History.
3. Slavery—Brazil—History. I. Hellwig, David J., 1937–   .
F2659.N4A34   1992
981'.00496—dc20   91-30852

Contents

Acknowledgments ix
Preface xi

INTRODUCTION: *The Myth of the Racial Paradise* 1

PART I: *The Myth Affirmed (1900–1940)* 15

1. "Brazilian Visitors in Norfolk" 21
2. "Brazil vs. United States" 23
3. "Brazil and the Black Race" 26
4. [W.E.B. Du Bois], "Brazil" 31
5. "Opportunities in Brazil: South American Country Offers First Hand Knowledge of the Solving of the Race Question" 35
6. [Cyril V. Briggs], "Brazil" 37
7. [Associated Negro Press], "Wonderful Opportunities Offered in Brazil for Thrifty People of All Races" 40
8. L. H. Stinson, "South America and Its Prospects in 1920" 44
9. E. R. James, "Brazil as I Found It" 47

10. Frank St. Claire, "Sidelights on Brazil Racial
    Conditions" 51
11. Robert S. Abbott, "My Trip Through South
    America" 55
12. William Pickens, "Sightseeing in South America" 82

PART II: *The Myth Debated (1940–1965)* 85

13. Ollie Stewart, "The Color Line in South America's
    Largest Republic" 91
14. James W. Ivy, "Stewart in Error; No Color Line
    in Brazil" 109
15. Letter by W.E.B. Du Bois to Edward Weeks,
    Atlanta, Georgia, October 2, 1941 117
16. E. Franklin Frazier, "Brazil Has No Race Problem" 121
17. E. Franklin Frazier, "A Comparison of Negro–
    White Relations in Brazil and the United States" 131
18. Thomas Roy Peyton, Excerpt from *Quest for
    Dignity: An Autobiography of a Negro Doctor* 137
19. George S. Schuyler, "Brazilian Color Bias Growing
    More Rampant" 145
20. Lorenzo D. Turner, "The Negro in Brazil" 159

PART III: *The Myth Rejected (1965–)* 167

21. Angela M. Gilliam, "From Roxbury to Rio—and
    Back in a Hurry" 173
22. Leslie B. Rout, Jr., "Brazil: Study in Black,
    Brown and Beige" 182
23. Cleveland Donald, Jr., "Equality in Brazil:
    Confronting Reality" 198
24. Richard L. Jackson, " 'Mestizaje' vs. Black Identity:
    The Color Crisis in Latin America" 216

25. Niani (Dee Brown), "Black Consciousness vs. Racism in Brazil" 225
26. Gloria Calomee, "Brazil and the Blacks of South America" 249
27. Rachel Jackson Christmas, "In Harmony with Brazil's African Pulse" 253

Acknowledgments

THIS COLLECTION is a product of more than a decade of research on the ties among African Americans, Latin Americans, and Afro-Latin Americans. In a sense it reflects my entire academic career going back to undergraduate days as a history major at the University of New Mexico in the late 1950s. There I began the study of Latin America with two distinguished historians, France V. Scholes and Edwin Lieuwen. My interest in Afro-Latin America had its origins in a summer seminar with Carl Degler at Stanford University in 1964; it was there that I first read the provocative books by Frank Tannenbaum, *Slave and Citizen: The Negro in the Americas* (1946), and Stanley Elkins, *Slavery: A Problem in American Institutional and Intellectual Life* (1959). My more formal study of Latin-American and African-American history took place more than a decade later as a graduate student at Syracuse University with Robert J. Shafer and Otey M. Scruggs.

The research that resulted in this book began while I was a National Endowment for the Humanities (NEH) Fellow at Brown University in 1977–78, where I had the good fortune to work with Rhett Jones and Anani Dzidzienyo. The encouragement of Charles Wagley during a NEH summer seminar on Brazil at the University of Florida in 1981 and that of Thomas Skidmore in subsequent years has helped me endure. A Fulbright-Hays Seminar Abroad program in Brazil during the summer of 1989 made the subject matter of the research come alive.

Like all books, this is a collaborative project, and I owe much to those family members, colleagues, librarians, and teachers who encouraged this white American in his study of the African-American experience and of Latin America.

Preface

THE MAIN PURPOSE of this book is to contribute to the study of African-American social thought. Black Americans, like all people, have sought to make sense of the events and trends occurring beyond their immediate environments for themselves and others. Most studies of African-American attitudes toward and involvement in international issues, and especially black views regarding people of color elsewhere, have concentrated on Africa. Little has been published regarding the north–south linkages among people of African descent in the New World. With the exception of Haiti and, to a limited extent, Cuba, African-American interest in Latin America has not been explored in detail.

Brazil has long been of special interest to African Americans. Despite the fact that it was the last nation to abolish slavery, Brazil has traditionally been viewed by its citizens and by foreign observers as a social democracy or racial paradise. Scholars and other observers have looked to Brazil for insights that might be applied toward solving racial problems in the United States. For most of the twentieth century, African Americans, including a large number of black leaders, preached the lessons of the Brazilian experience to skeptical, if not hostile, whites, many of whom often believed that racial antipathy and the subsequent pattern of fear and separation were inevitable, perhaps innate. More important, they used the image of Brazil as an open, colorblind utopia for people of color to instill hope among those who, long after the legal abolition of slavery, lived in social, economic, and political servitude. Some black leaders were so inspired by the Brazilian situation—or so discouraged about prospects in their land of birth—that they saw in Brazil a potential refuge, a proud black homeland in the emerging colossus of the South rather than in the geographically and culturally more remote Africa.

The image of Brazil as a racial paradise in effect became a myth that served important functions for black Americans, very few of whom in the nineteenth or early twentieth century had visited South America. By the middle of the twentieth century, however, some prominent African Americans began to question the prevailing image. Particularly important was the work of social scientists and journalists who visited Brazil and observed the subtleties of race and class firsthand. Interestingly, though, some of the brightest and best-trained black scholars endorsed the myth—or at least its essence—even when their observations and sometimes their personal experiences contradicted it. By the mid-1960s, however, the image of the social democracy had crumbled, especially among younger scholars who had lived or traveled in Latin America and who interpreted what they saw in terms of the nationalistic ideology stimulated by the slow pace of change in the United States and the emergence of people of color elsewhere in the world. The conviction that the condition of people of African descent in the United States was not unique and that the solution to the plight of African

Americans was linked to the future of formerly enslaved or colonized nonwhite peoples throughout the world led black Americans to rethink their own situation and that of people of color elsewhere, including Latin America.

Black Americans came to see Brazilian society as full of all-too-familiar contradictions and dangers for people of color rather than as a model for emulation. Indeed, the myth of the paradise began to give way to nightmarish possibilities. Some blacks feared that as the United States destroyed Jim Crow and as white behavior and attitudes changed toward greater acceptance, the United States might become more like Brazil, where, despite the lack of overt racial violence and discrimination and the acceptance of intermarriage, Afro-Brazilians as a group lacked a sense of pride in their Africanness as well as wealth, power, and office.

This book consists of observations of race relations in Brazil from the first decade of the century through the 1980s. While writings by some of the outstanding black scholars of this century, notably W.E.B. Du Bois and E. Franklin Frazier, are included, most of the articles were written for general audiences and are short and personal in tone. The book will be of greatest value to students of African-American history; it should also interest those studying Latin America as well as social scientists specializing in the dynamics of ethnicity, color, and class. The insights that African Americans provide into Brazilian race relations are unique and valuable to all citizens of the United States as well as to Latin Americans, many of whom are currently reassessing race relations in their societies.

INTRODUCTION

The Myth of the Racial Paradise

As the nation with the second largest population of people of African descent in the world, Brazil has long attracted students of slavery and race relations. Numbers alone, however, do not account for the attention given by scholars to the past and present status of Afro-Brazilians. Scholars and nonscholars alike see Brazil as highlighting the contrast between Latin America and Anglo America on matters of race. Both the United States and Brazil are properly seen as racially and ethnically diverse, but traditionally Brazil has been viewed at home and abroad as a very different society from the United States. So great are the differences that Brazil has often been portrayed as a social democracy or racial paradise. The uniqueness of Brazil's treatment of slaves and their twentieth-century descendants is a key component of Brazil's national image and a source of great pride. Despite the fact that nonwhites remain clustered at the bottom of the social structure more than a century after abolition, Afro-Brazilians are still purported to be virtually unencumbered by the barriers that black Americans have faced.

Brazilian Slavery

African slaves were introduced into Brazil in the middle of the sixteenth century. In part because the government ordered the destruction of records pertaining to slavery shortly after the abolition of the institution in 1888, the number of Africans brought to Brazil is difficult to determine. Most historians estimate that between 3.5 and 5 million African slaves reached Brazilian shores, a number many times greater than the approximately 427,000 sent to the United States.

As in the rest of the New World, colonial plantations and mines in Brazil were completely dependent on a steady flow of cheap slave labor. Until the mid-1600s, most slaves toiled in the sugar cane fields in Northeast Brazil. In the following century they provided labor for the coffee farms, first in the Northeast and later in Rio de Janeiro and São Paulo. They also dug for gold and diamonds in the mines of Minas Gerais in the 1700s and 1800s. By the time slavery was finally outlawed, most slaves were engaged in domestic or service jobs or in agriculture in the rapidly developing Southeast.

Brazil's reputation for harmonious race relations is closely tied to its slave past. Traditionally, Brazilian and American scholars have emphasized the uniqueness of Brazilian slavery, particularly its mildness and humaneness. These scholars have argued that the complex system of social and psychological relationships developed on the sugar plantations of Northeast Brazil mitigated the violence, physical and psychological, that characterized slavery in the British colonies. They stress the Portuguese cultural heritage, especially the nation's extensive contacts over the centuries with people of diverse backgrounds. This heritage, reinforced by the teachings of the Roman Catholic Church, imperial legislation protecting the slaves, and the dearth of European women in the colony, fostered greater appreciation of the humanness of those enslaved.[1] This resulted in a greater tendency of Portuguese males to intermix with Amerindian and African females than in colonial America, more frequent manumission, and greater toleration of free Negroes, a large percentage of whom were mulattoes.[2]

Race Relations Since Abolition

According to those who adhere to the traditional interpretation of Brazil's past, the way in which abolition occurred has also contributed to the modern record of racial harmony. They emphasize that the process was a gradual one, free of violence and regional conflict. The final cessation of the slave trade in 1851 and the Free Womb Law of 1871, granting freedom to children of slave mothers at maturity, assured extinction of the institution in a generation or two. The freeing of all slaves through the "Golden Law" of May 13, 1888—decreed by Princess Isabel, who served as regent while her father, Emperor Dom Pedro II, was in Europe—symbolizes the enlightened path Brazil followed in removing the curse of slavery.

The relative ease with which slavery was abolished and the ongoing amalgamation of the races, according to the traditional interpretation, created a postemancipation environment for ex-slaves dramatically different from that in the United States, where by the 1890s a racially based caste system in effect perpetuated the old slave order politically, economically, and socially. Antimiscegenation laws, segregation, race riots, and lynchings were and continue to be foreign to Brazil. Since neither Jim Crow nor other characteristics of race relations in the United States took root in Brazil, the nation today has no need for civil rights laws and social programs aimed at advancing the well-being of the descendants of slaves. Indeed, in Brazil citizens do not identify themselves in racial terms; all think of themselves as Brazilians and are treated accordingly.

But even the most vocal proponents of what has come to be known as the "myth of the racial paradise" acknowledge that the nation is not totally free of prejudice and that acts of discrimination occur, such as the exclusion of dark-skinned Brazilians and tourists from first-class hotels and swank restaurants. But such phenomena are typically discounted, viewed as exceptional and as evidence of alien—usually American—influences. The facts that the complexion of *favelados* (shantytown dwellers) is darker than that of those who live in upper-income neighborhoods and that few Afro-Brazilians can be found on university campuses are commonly dismissed as consequences of class-based barriers to social mobility and not as manifestations of racism. So strong is the desire of white as well as many dark-skinned Brazilians to adhere to the belief in racial democracy that those who raise the issue of racism or in some other way express racial consciousness are seen as "un-Brazilian" and as dangerous deviants who threaten the unity and strength of Brazil by introducing inappropriate foreign perspectives.

Despite its pervasiveness, the image of Brazil as a social or racial democracy has not been without its critics, at home and abroad. Especially since the 1950s, virtually every element in the set of beliefs and assumptions that make up the myth of the racial paradise has been seriously challenged.[3] Contemporary students of comparative slave systems in the New World, for example, tend to stress the similarities and brutality of slavery regardless of location. They point out that in some ways Brazilian slavery was, if anything, harsher than slavery in the United States: slaves were worked harder and fed less, resulting in much shorter life spans; and fewer slaves had the opportunity to marry and raise families. Slaves commonly committed suicide, and insurrections among them were far more frequent than in the United States. Portuguese laws and church decrees were typically ignored when they interfered with the self-interest of plantation and mine owners. Most race mixture took place outside marriage and can more appropriately be explained in terms of the power relationship of European males and Amerindian and African women than in terms of Portuguese culture and temperament. The notion that Brazilian slavery was qualitatively different from other systems of servitude, critics argue, had its origins in nineteenth-century Brazilian efforts to defend slavery and has been perpetuated by twentieth-century elites seeking to minimize social discord.

The extinction of slavery in the second half of the nineteenth century is also viewed differently by revisionist scholars. Rather than emphasizing the gradual and smooth transition from a slave to a free labor system, they note the opposition to abolition, the role the British played in curtailing the slave trade, and the resistance of slaves to the system. The overthrow of Emperor Dom Pedro II within months of the final abolition of slavery, along with the recruitment of Europeans in the late nineteenth and early twentieth century to replace the freed slaves, also challenges the picture of a society eager to embrace ex-slaves as equals. While no system of segregation, legal or otherwise, was introduced into postemancipation Brazil, neither was there any effort to assist former slaves in making the transition out of bondage. The bulk of freed slaves remained dependent upon white plantation owners; others migrated to cities, especially Rio de Janeiro and São Paulo, where they faced competition from immigrant workers. Abruptly cut loose from the paternalism of the slave system and thrown into an increasingly competitive free labor market, former slaves were ill fitted to prosper in the emerging capitalist, urban society of modern Brazil.

Consequently, in today's Brazil as in the past, Afro-Brazilians—*pretos* (blacks) and *pardos* (browns) alike—occupy a distinctly subordinate place in society. Few are found in high positions in the church, the educational system, or government. The cost of being nonwhite can be seen in average incomes, years of school, life expectancy, and housing. Black workers continue to be concentrated mostly in agriculture, construction, and services. A disproportionate number reside in the underdeveloped, agricultural Northeast, where educational and occupational opportunities are much more limited than in the Southeast. As in the United States, nonwhites are as underrepresented in the professions as they are overrepresented in prisons. They are either left out of the popular media or portrayed in stereotypic ways. Only in sports, notably soccer, and in other forms of entertainment do they compete with some semblance of equality with whites.

Critics and supporters of the myth of racial democracy agree that in some ways Brazilian race relations differ from those in the United States. Both acknowledge the existence of a racial continuum in Brazil, in contrast to the bipolar, black or white classification system used in North America. Most agree that miscegenation is both more common and more socially acceptable in Brazil than in the United States. Virtually everyone agrees that the kind of white supremacist ideology and organizations and the overt violence found in the United States are foreign to the South American republic. Consensus also exists on the greater impact of African culture in contemporary Brazil, especially in cuisine, religion, and music, than in the United States. In effect, most observers see Brazil as more truly a melting pot—both physically and culturally—than the United States and most other Western Hemisphere nations.

While some view these features of Brazilian society as evidence of benign race relations, others interpret them quite differently, contending that they merely create an illusion of a racially harmonious and just society. In particular, critics argue that blackness, in both its cultural and physical dimensions, is given less value than whiteness in Brazil. European and U.S. culture is studied and emulated while Africanisms in Brazilian culture are largely ignored or portrayed as mere vestiges of the past. The African heritage of Brazil as well as current developments in Africa merit little attention in the nation's schools. Dark-skinned Brazilians often identify themselves as having lighter or more European features than they do in reality while "white" Brazilians acknowledge their African ancestry only if there is no risk of being identified as anything other than Caucasian.

Brazil's population today is so thoroughly mixed that it is difficult to determine the racial derivation of most people with precision, a problem compounded by the desire of many people of African descent to define themselves as white. According to a 1987 household survey, 43 percent of Brazilians are black or of mixed race, with only 5.6 percent of this group recorded as *pretos*.[4] Many scholars—and the small but growing community of Afro-Brazilian activists—view these figures as understated. Some assert that as many as 80 percent of Brazil's 150 million citizens have some African ancestry. Certainly, were North American criteria applied, more than half of the nation would be classified as "Negro."

The belief that Brazil is in the process of becoming one people, a new meta-race born in the tropics, is seen by many Brazilian and foreign critics as a rejection of both the Indianness and Africanness of Brazil in favor of *branqueamento* ("bleaching" or "whitening"), purging the society of the presumably "damaging" impact of nonwhite "blood."[5] Furthermore, it fosters an "etiquette of race relations"[6] in which discussion of racial issues is socially unacceptable. Dark people who adhere to the ideal of whitening may seek to marry someone lighter or think of themselves not as Afro-Brazilians but just as Brazilians. This lack of racial consciousness stifles efforts to identify racist behavior and policies and retards the creation of organizations dedicated to the protection and advancement of black and brown citizens. Thus, critics of the myth of the racial paradise claim, the racial status quo is effectively maintained.

African-American Perspectives

The selections in this book provide a unique insight into both Brazilian race relations and the social thought of African Americans. As foreigners, black Americans have been free of the influence of Brazilian beliefs and assumptions. Their views have been molded instead by their experiences as citizens of a nation that often has refused to acknowledge their citizenship and treated them as aliens or nonhuman. This marginal status created what W.E.B. Du Bois, in his 1903 classic *The Souls of Black Folks*, called a "dual consciousness." Black Americans, he and others have argued, possess a perspective that is shaped both by the experiences they share with other Americans and by their unique experiences as slaves and later as second-class citizens. Thus the way in which African Americans interpreted the Brazilian racial environment was likely to be different from that of the dominant group of Americans as well as from that of Brazilians, both white and nonwhite.

While both at the beginning of this century and during the past generation African-American reactions to Brazilian race relations have been marked by a high level of consistency, contemporary black Americans interpret Brazilian race relations very differently than was the pattern before World War II. The shift from an overwhelmingly positive to a sharply critical perspective may be attributed in part to greater knowledge of Brazil among a better-educated people who have had the opportunity to read revisionist attacks on the traditional portrayal of black–white relations in Brazil or, in some cases, to travel in South America. As African Americans learn more about Brazil they have been confronted with disparities in the condition of blacks and whites that resemble patterns at home. While they may applaud the persistence of African culture in northeastern Brazil and, to a lesser extent, elsewhere in Brazil, they deplore the paucity of black studies programs in universities and the general lack of value given to blackness in a society that still turns its back to Africa and its African heritage. As they study Afro-Brazil, black Americans learn of the creation of the Frente Negra Brazileira (Brazilian Negro Front) in 1931 in São Paulo, the Teatro Experimental do Negro (Negro Experimental Theater) movement founded by the journalist Abdias do Nascimento in Rio de Janeiro in 1944, and the militant Movimento Negro Unificado (Black Unified Movement), created in São Paulo in 1978, all of which by their mere existence contradict the longstanding myth of Brazil as a racial democracy. The strong opposition each of these groups faced from the government suggests to some, at least, that dominant-group Brazilians have been even less receptive to black demands than have white Americans.

But for the most part the dramatic transformation

in African-American views is a product of a variety of changes in U.S. society at large and within black America during the twentieth century. The despair of African Americans living in the first decades of the century, a period one historian has referred to as the nadir of the Negro,[7] contributed to the affirmation of the myth of the racial paradise. With its absence of racial violence and legal segregation, Brazil represented a clearly superior alternative to America's pattern of race relations. The Great Migration out of the rural South, World War II, the rise of anticolonial movements, and the civil rights movement served to undermine Jim Crow, raise aspirations, and foster race consciousness; they also stimulated a reassessment of Brazil at mid-century. The subsequent decline of the civil rights movement, the reassertion of black nationalism, and the growing awareness of the role of class-related factors in perpetuating the subordinate status of people of color in the United States have strongly influenced African Americans' rejection of the idealized image of Brazil since the mid-1960s.

NOTES

1. Among the best-known of these studies are Gilberto Freyre, *The Masters and the Slaves: A Study in the Development of Brazilian Civilization* (New York, 1946); Frank Tannenbaum, *Slave and Citizen: The Negro in the Americas* (New York, 1946); Stanley M. Elkins, *Slavery: A Problem in American Institutional and Intellectual Life* (New York, 1959).

2. Carl N. Degler, in his influential study *Neither Black Nor White: Slavery and Race Relations in Brazil and the United States* (New York, 1971), emphasized the considerable opportunity for upward mobility for "mixed blood" people in

Brazil, in contrast to the United States, by way of a "mulatto escape hatch."

3. Some of the revisionist works are Charles R. Boxer, *The Golden Age in Brazil, 1695–1750: Growing Pains of a Colonial Society* (Berkeley, 1962); Anani Dzidzienyo, *The Position of Blacks in Brazilian Society* (London, 1971); Florestan Fernandes, *The Negro in Brazilian Society* (New York, 1969); Carlos A. Hasenbalg, *Discriminação e Desigualdades Raciais no Brasil* (Rio de Janeiro, 1979); Getavio Ianni, *Escravidão e Racismo* (São Paulo, 1978); Abdias do Nascimento, *O Genocidio do Negro Brasileiro* (Rio de Janeiro, 1978); Stanley Stein, *Vassouras: A Brazilian Coffee County, 1850–1900* (Cambridge, Mass., 1957). An excellent recent collection of essays, all of which challenge the traditional image of race relations in Brazil, is Pierre-Michel Fontaine, ed., *Race, Class and Power in Brazil* (Los Angeles, 1985).

4. The distinction between *pretos* and *pardos*, while important in the Brazilian context, is not an important one in the essays included in this book since the authors follow the North American practice of referring to all people of African descent as "Negroes," "blacks," or "Afro-Brazilians."

5. Brazilian efforts to Europeanize and "whiten" Brazil are discussed in Jeffrey D. Needell, *A Tropical Belle Epoque: Elite Culture and Society in Turn-of-the-Century Rio de Janeiro* (Cambridge and New York, 1987); and Thomas E. Skidmore, *Black into White: Race and Nationality in Brazilian Thought* (New York, 1974).

6. A phrase used by Dzidzienyo, *Position of Blacks in Brazilian Society*, 5.

7. Rayford W. Logan, *The Negro in American Life and Thought: The Nadir, 1877–1901* (New York, 1954).

PART I

The Myth Affirmed (1900–1940)

THE ESSAYS IN Part I express the favorable image most African Americans held of Brazil in the early twentieth century, a period of economic and political stagnation for black Americans. In 1905 the editor of the *Colored American Magazine*, published in New York City, used an incident in Norfolk, Virginia, involving Brazilian sailors of mixed ancestry to attack a key article of racial thought in the United States: the fear of miscegenation (Selection 1). The essays responding to ex-President Theodore Roosevelt's visit to Brazil in the fall of 1913 and to his report on blacks in Brazil, all published in major African-American journals, affirm that the U.S. pattern of race relations was not universal and that, as a Brazilian statesman warned Roosevelt, "The course the American people are pursuing toward the Black man is a most dangerous one" (Selections 2–4).

Selection 5 is an early statement endorsing the migration of black Americans to Brazil. Emigrationist sentiments grew after World War I with the resurgence of racial violence and the frustration of dreams nourished by America's involvement in the war and enhanced economic opportunities for blacks. The persistence of the racial status quo fostered a rebirth of black nationalism, best symbolized by Marcus Garvey and the Universal Negro Improvement Association. Most who envisioned a better life outside the United States looked to Africa, but some favored Brazil, a theme in Selections 6 through 10. Although they acknowledged that money and marketable skills were essential for success in Brazil, many nationalists gave the South American republic a strong endorsement, reflecting both loss of faith in the possibility for equality in the United States and acceptance of the positive portrayal of Brazilian race relations.

Selection 11, the longest in Part I, is of special interest because of the prominence of its author, Robert S. Abbott, and of the *Chicago Defender*, the newspaper he owned and published. When Abbott and his wife visited South America in 1923 the *Defender* was perhaps the most important of all black newspapers. Abbott was a practical, down-to-earth businessman and a community leader in a city with a large and, thanks to southern migrants, still-growing black population. He was also a leading opponent of Garvey. Nevertheless, he urged his readers to look to Brazil both as a refuge from racism and as a new frontier offering economic opportunities in abundance, especially for those with a trade or an entrepreneurial bent. Like other proponents of emigration, Abbott ignored or discounted actions by Brazil designed to prevent immigration by people of African descent.[1]

The closing essay in Part I, by William Pickens, was inspired by President-elect Hoover's trip to South America in late 1928. In stressing what South America could teach the United States, Pickens, like the other commentators, painted an uncritically positive image of social relations in Brazil. Virtually without exception in the early twentieth century—as well as in the rare nineteenth-century references—whenever African Americans mentioned Brazil, the position of the Afro-Brazilian was the focus. Those observers who had firsthand knowledge of the country, as well as those who did not, cited Brazil as proof that racial antipathy was not inevitable in societies with a heritage of racially based slavery. The United States could learn much from Brazil; if it refused to change—as seemed to be the situation in post–World War I America—blacks would be wise to establish new homes in South America.

NOTE

1. African-American interest in Brazil and the resistance of the Brazilian government to black immigration are discussed in Teresa Meade and Gregory Alonso Pirio, "In Search of the Afro-American 'Eldorado': Attempts by North American Blacks to Enter Brazil in the 1920s," *Luso-Brazilian Review* 25 (Summer 1988), 85–110.

1.
"Brazilian Visitors in Norfolk"

ON JUNE 24TH a number of Brazilian sailors and soldiers went abroad at Norfolk, Virginia. In their carousings they stepped into a fashionable café; and a panic almost ensued; indeed a riot was scarcely averted. The South Americans were taken for Negroes, insolent, intruding and social equality-hunting, and it was decided to make sure meat of them to quench the growing thirst of our Southern parents, brothers and friends. The timely speech of Lieutenant Florente, who assured the mob that his friends and he were not aware that they were causing confusion, saved both the visitors from destruction and the mob unnecessary exertion. The party withdrew from the café, and found quarters and hospitality at the Monticello Hotel.

The Brazilian Consul at Norfolk assured the not yet convinced and impassioned populace that his friends were of Spanish descent, and further, that they were "educated and cultured," and perhaps brave, "naval officers."

The truth is, these men were Portuguese and Brazilians, who were no more of Spain than the writer is of Palestine;

From *Colored American Magazine* 9 (August 1905), 406–7.

and both assertions are of doubtful force, and should be taken slowly, because in this great, wide world, where men and women of all countries and bloods are meeting, and associating and intermarrying, who shall say what blood it is that does not course through his veins?

There are millions of Negroes in Brazil; amalgamation is as common there now as it was in the southern part of the United States before the War of the Rebellion. Social equality with the beautiful women of Negro descent is courted by the Spanish [sic] noblemen of Brazil. Marriages have ensued in thousands of instances and the children of this union are the backbone of the culture, character and capital of both countries.

Those naval officers who appeared at Norfolk were the descendants of both the Castilian blood, and the blood of those who occupied Spain for seven centuries; during which time they erected the gigantic and magnificent buildings which are now the wonder of the world, and laid the foundation for the startling inventions which have come out of Madrid, both of which testify to a genius for conceptions, and a power of execution, which the Anglo-Saxon has never touched in all his strivings and imitations.

Negroes? Certainly they were. Half of the population of the South have Negro blood in its [sic] veins. The South has produced no man of genius, of whom it has not been said, and is much believed, and perhaps can be proved, that he was of mixed origin.

No South American dare set his foot on these shores, and deny that either upon his maternal or paternal side, he does not come of the blood which founded and ruled the world's civilization for thousands of years, and which is fast coming again unto its own.

2.
"Brazil vs. United States"

THEODORE ROOSEVELT, in his series on South America, writes, in the February *Outlook*, on "Brazil and the Negro."[1] The article is prefaced by this note from the editors: "It may be noted that in this article Mr. Roosevelt is not attempting either to justify or condemn the Brazilian attitude toward the Negro as contrasted with that of the United States, but simply to set forth clearly what the Brazilian attitude is in the fact." After reading Mr. Roosevelt's splendidly written article, teeming with facts uncontrovertible concerning the status of the colored man in Brazil, and then comparing their treatment here in the United States, the full meaning of the preface dawns upon you. The *Outlook* has many readers who have many views, and to offend even the least of them is not their policy. There is little or no prejudice in Brazil; therefore the problem, as we term it, is being solved in the only possible and effective way of solving it, by absorption. The intermarriage of the races is a common occurrence, a man or woman being solely judged on their individual merit, upon their standing in life, the color of their skin playing little

From the *Chicago Defender*, February 28, 1914. Reprinted by permission of the *Chicago Daily Defender*.

part. Americans with their unjust deep-seated prejudices rebel at this means of settlement, and the result is that the chasm between the races is growing wider and wider and the problem is becoming more complex. The colored man is not seeking to lose his identity, is not seeking for social equality, but the white man is throwing up every barrier for fear that he may change his mind. What the outcome of all of this is going to be is perhaps best prophesied by a Brazilian statesman, who said: "You of the United States are keeping the blacks as an entirely separate element, and you are not treating them in a way that fosters their self respect. They will remain a menacing element in your civilization, permanent, and perhaps even after a while a growing element. With us the question tends to disappear, because the blacks themselves tend to disappear and become absorbed. In a century there will not be any Negroes in Brazil, whereas you will have twenty or thirty million of them. Then for you there will be a real and very uncomfortable problem, while for us the problem in its most menacing phase will have disappeared." It can readily be seen that the ideals of the United States and of Brazil are wholly different regarding the treatment of the colored people and it does not take much thought to decide which is the better. It takes the American people, as wise as they think they are, a long time to get their eyes open to the fact that they are standing in their own light; that they are letting their prejudices stand in the way of their better judgment; that they are letting a disgruntled semi-rebel element of the South speak and act for them, with the result that the whole country is having the finger of scorn pointed at them for the unchristian-like way they are dealing with the people within their gates whose skin is of a darker hue. Strange they cannot see they must inevitably reap what they sow. Our government is long on investigating, so it might be well to send a commission to Brazil and report if they find conditions as Colonel Roosevelt describes, and if so bring back a working model and give a demonstration.

NOTE

1. Roosevelt's articles, based on the tour he took of Latin America in the fall of 1913, appeared in *Outlook* between November 29, 1913, and March 21, 1914. "Brazil and the Negro" was published in vol. 106 (February 21, 1914), 409–11.

3.
"Brazil and the Black Race"

Col. Roosevelt in his tour through South America has been using his eyes to good effect and has given his observations in a series of articles to the readers of the *Outlook*. What he has stated in his last article is of more than passing interest to us as a race, especially his travels through Brazil, which leads us to compare the attitude of Brazil to that of this country in its treatment of the Black race. Both countries were at one time slave holding countries, that of Brazil owing to its diamond industry had possibly more slaves than this, and their treatment was possibly more cruel than that of this country. There was this redeeming feature in theirs. Families were not separated there as here; when there was an exchange of owners the family was sold and not the individual as in this country. In 1871 the Brazilian government decreed the gradual emancipation of all held in bondage. In 1888 there was not a slave in that country. All had become free. This was twenty-five years after President Lincoln declared the freedom of the slaves, January 1st, '63. But it was not until the ratification of the thirteenth amendment on the eighteenth

From the *Philadelphia Tribune*, March 14, 1914.

of December, '65, that slavery may be said to have ceased to exist within the confines of this country.

It is from this period that the contrast in the treatment of the two countries of the Black race is to be compared. In this country since the close of the Civil War, notwithstanding the ratification of the thirteenth, fourteenth and fifteenth amendments, the policy of this Nation, especially in the South, has been to deny to the Black man all the rights guaranteed to him by those amendments and this prejudice has extended from that section to the North, East and West. So much is this the case that in any city in these sections where any considerable portion of our people reside their condition is little better than serfs or peons. They are simply considered pariahs in the land of their birth, segregation and ostracism is their lot, all avenues to their advancement in the trades or in any occupation that demands skill is closed to them. The same may be said in regard to professional and literary pursuits, and when one of this race succeeds it is due to sheer perseverance. This ostracism has been a benefit to him in many cases as it has aroused his latent powers and has led him to establish churches, schools, colleges and hospitals for his use that otherwise would not have been thought of. In the social world his limits and bounds are even more restricted than what he finds in the business world. He is debarred from all cafés, hotels and places of entertainment and when admitted to any of them he is segregated to a special place as if he was affected with leprosy or some other infectious or contagious disease, while on the other hand aliens from the time of their landing have more rights and privileges than he does. This prejudice has become so great that even in the common pursuits of life he is gradually being crowded out and when he is fortunate to secure employment he is paid much less than is the white laborer for the same class of work, and this in a land which boasts of being the land of the free and the home of the brave, all because his skin is of a darker hue than that of his more fortunate brother of the other race. A few, a very few, escape some of this humiliation on account of their lighter color. . . .

In Brazil, as Col. Roosevelt states in his article, this question of color does not exist there, though the date of their enfranchisement is of a more recent date than that of this country. There a man is judged by personal merit. There is no blank wall of prejudice that faces him. All the opportunities of life are open to him. If there is a failure it is by the individual and not from any prejudice on the part of the dominant class to keep him down or to deny to him the rights of a man and a citizen of Brazil. There is no line of demarcation drawn anywhere in the business world, the mechanic arts, in the artisan class or in the social world. He is as free to enter these as any member of the other race. All depends upon the merit that is within him.

Col. Roosevelt as may be supposed was surprised to find such a condition of affairs in a country that within a comparatively recent period had manumitted its slaves. He found no separation into classes. He found colored professors in the national schools as well as in the military schools. He found colored men expounding law and administering justice in the several courts of the country. There was not the least appearance of segregation, not even in that closer relation in life—the marital state—the marriage of white women to black men, or black women and white men was not considered a crime. It was more favored than opposed by both classes in consequence of which lynching was unknown there. So great was Col. Roosevelt surprised that he commented upon it. He was informed by a leading statesman of that country in these words, "The policy of my country is this, our efforts are directed to absorb the colored class of our people, and not have them to absorb us. We do not favor segregation or ostracism, as is pursued by citizens of your country. Our aim is to make him homogeneous, and by these means he becomes a part of us. The course the American people are pursuing towards the Black man is a most dangerous one. By your segregation and ostracism, you are making of this class bitter foes to your national life. You will remember that the Black race is a virile race and is increasing in number yearly. Within a few centuries they will be most potent in numbers, in influence and wealth and with a bitter hatred for your people for the humiliation they have been forced to submit to and for this they will wreak their vengeance upon you, while with us in this country we will know no color line as the Black man will be completely absorbed."

Col. Roosevelt further states that in visiting one of the national galleries of paintings his attention was directed to a painting that caused him to pause. It was one showing the evolution of the Black race, the painting represented four generations of that race. The first represented the Black man pure and simple, then follows each generation, each becoming lighter than the last, finally in the fourth there is seen one in whom there is not a trace of the Negro race, showing how gradual this absorption had taken place. What has been stated by Col. Roosevelt in his article in the *Outlook* is not startling. The same state of things can be seen in other South American States, in the West Indies, in those islands governed by England, France and Denmark. It also can be seen to a great extent in Continental Europe. It is only in this country that this state of affairs exists.

Unless there comes a change on the part of the dominant race in its treatment of the Black race in this country in the recognition of his rights as a man and as a citizen with all the privileges that pertain to it, a condition of affairs will come in this country as predicted by this Brazilian statesman. This race is daily smarting from the wrongs they are suffering, the deprivation of privileges to which they are entitled and they will not be slow to right these wrongs when the opportunity comes for them to do so.

If the dominant race is wise they should follow the example that the Brazilians have set them to absorb the Black race and not let that race absorb them. Unless they do so, this condition of affairs will come and must come.

4.
[W.E.B. Du Bois], "Brazil"

> *William Edward Burghardt Du Bois (1868–1963) was born in Great Barrington, Massachusetts, and educated at Fisk University and Harvard University, where he earned a Ph.D. in history in 1895, the first doctorate awarded by the university to an African American. He subsequently taught sociology at Atlanta University; played a key role in the creation of the National Association for the Advancement of Colored People (NAACP); founded* The Crisis, *which he edited for more than two decades; and published dozens of books, including* The Philadelphia Negro *(1899),* The Souls of Black Folk *(1903), and* Black Reconstruction in America *(1935), as well as autobiographical works and novels.*

AS A MAGNIFICENT essay in valiant timidity we recommend Mr. Theodore Roosevelt's "Brazil and the Negro" in the *Outlook*. The story which he has to tell is simple: There are in Brazil 8,300,000 Negroes and mulattoes; 3,700,000 Indian and mixed Indian-whites and

From *The Crisis* 7 (April 1914), 286–87. Reprinted by permission of the Crisis Publishing Co., New York, New York.

8,000,000 persons of European descent. All these elements are fusing into one light mulatto race.

These are simple facts. Mr. Roosevelt has hitherto rather ostentatiously avoided them. He visited Rio de Janeiro, with a Negroid population in the hundred thousands, and almost overlooked them; he visited Bahia, if we mistake not, which has more Negroes than any city in the world, and quite forgot them.

At last, however, Mr. Roosevelt coyly approaches his subject. The editors warn away the frivolous with these protesting italics: "It may be noted that in this article Mr. Roosevelt is not attempting to justify or condemn the Brazilian attitude toward the Negro as contrasted with that of the United States, but simply to set forth clearly what the Brazilian attitude is in fact."

Mr. Roosevelt then, in characteristic fashion, states three facts and two falsehoods.

The facts are:

1. Brazil is absorbing the Negro race.
2. There is no color bar to advancement.
3. There is no social bar to advancement, but the mass of full-blooded Negroes are still in the lower social class.

Then come the falsehoods:

1. The best men in the United States believe "in treating each man of whatever color absolutely on his worth as a man, allowing him full opportunity to achieve the success warranted by his ability and integrity, and giving to him the full measure of respect to which that success entitles him." This is not so and Mr. Roosevelt knows it is not so. The best men in the United States believe that their "civilization"

can only be maintained by compelling all persons of Negro descent to occupy an inferior place. The exceptions to this belief are negligible.
2. That the Brazilians regard the Negro element in their blood as "a slight weakening." What do Brazilians say as to this "slight weakening"? We quote from Dr. Jean Baptiste de Lacerda, director of the National Museum of Rio de Janeiro:

> The *metis*[1] of Brazil have given birth down to our own time to poets of no mean inspiration, painters, sculptors, distinguished musicians, magistrates, lawyers, eloquent orators, remarkable writers, medical men and engineers, who have been unrivaled in the technical skill and professional ability.
>
> The co-operation of the *metis* in the advance of Brazil is notorious and far from inconsiderable. They played the chief part during many years in Brazil in the campaign for the abolition of slavery. I could quote celebrated names of more than one of these *metis* who put themselves at the head of the literary movement. They fought with firmness and intrepidity in the press and on the platform. They faced with courage the greatest perils to which they were exposed in their struggle against the powerful slave owners, who had the protection of a conservative government. They gave evidence of sentiments of patriotism, self-denial and appreciation during the long campaign in Paraguay,[2] fighting heroically at the boarding of the ships in the canal battle of Riachuelo and in the attacks of the Brazilian army, on numerous occasions in the course of this long South American war. It was owing to their support that the republic was erected on the ruins of the empire.

And what of all this? Is it not a plea for intermarriage of whites and blacks in the United States? It is not. It is a plea for truth. It is a denial that lying will settle any human problem. Most white people in the United States prefer to marry white people. That is perfectly proper and defensible. Most colored people prefer to marry colored people. This is perfectly logical and commendable. These facts need no defense and need no proof. They are the easily understandable desire of both races.

But a vast number of people are not satisfied with such bare facts. They want to bolster them up with scientific lies and social insult. They want to scare and beat people into doing precisely what people would do without bogies and force, and the result is that they not only accomplish what they wish, but they also accomplish poverty, crime, prostitution, ignorance, lynching, mob violence and the ruin of democratic government for the unfortunate victims of their lies. All this is clear, but to expect Theodore Roosevelt to say it plainly without twistings and equivocations is to expect the millennium.

NOTES

1. A French word for a person of mixed racial background.
2. In the Paraguayan War of 1865–70, also known as the War of the Triple Alliance, Paraguay battled the combined armies of Brazil, Argentina, and Uruguay.

5.

"Opportunities in Brazil: South American Country Offers First Hand Knowledge of the Solving of the Race Question"

... IN HER OWN quiet way, Brazil has been progressive long before the European War caused America to seek another outlet for trade that could no longer cross the Atlantic. America just now begins to discover that the neighbors below the isthmus can entertain us very well while Europe is too busy to give us any of her time. It discovers among other interesting things that they have had race problems just as United States has had, is having, but that they in shorter time have gone far more toward a solution. Brazil did not free her slaves until ten years [sic] after we did, but already Brazil has had a mulatto President, and has now Cabinet officers, Judges, Congressmen, and military officers in every sense proportionate to the 50 percent of Negro population. In the Brazilian Congress, modeled after our own, for example, ninety of the one hundred sixty members bear evidence of Negro descent. Into the melting pot have been thrown indiscriminately Negroes, Portuguese, Indians and Spaniards and the result has not been black or white, but Brazilian, in just the same way that

From the *Baltimore Afro-American*, January 29, 1916. Reprinted by permission of the Afro-American Newspapers, Baltimore, Maryland.

Americans are made out of commingling of the polyglot of European emigrants that come to our shores.

From the above it would seem that Brazil would be to the educated colored man of today, what United States was to the European in 1850—a new land and a land of promise. From the point of view of climate and tradition, Brazil is the country peculiarly fitted to receive the colored man of this country, and offer him a vision of freedom and opportunity beyond his wildest dreams. This is the first great good for the Negro in closer relation with South America, and the second is little less in value.

Brazil offers a present and first hand evidence of the solution of the race problem by intermarriage. This example will not be lost on the American Negro. To him it is becoming plainer and plainer that the longer he remains a group within a group, the longer will the stronger group prey upon the weaker and less numerous. Far from admitting that miscegenation produces an offspring inferior to either, the conviction is spreading, founded on experience, that such offsprings are wise and stronger. . . .

6.
[Cyril V. Briggs], "Brazil"

> Cyril V. Briggs (1888–1953) migrated to the United States in 1905 from the island of Nevis in the British West Indies. He settled in New York City, where he worked as a reporter and editorial writer for The Amsterdam News before creating The Crusader in 1918. The magazine and the organization founded by Briggs and his associates, the African Blood Brotherhood, advocated black separatism, independence for Africa, and the destruction of capitalism.

THE CRUSADER is in receipt of several communications requesting information in re the fare to Brazil and "the inducements, if any, that are offered to immigrants by the Brazilian Government."

The second-class fare by the Brazilian-Lloyd for passage from New York to Bahia is one hundred and eighty-five dollars ($185). First class, three hundred and fifteen dollars ($315). . . . For families or groups of ten or more a discount is allowed by the steamship lines. For children between the ages of two and twelve the charge is half the fare of an adult in any of the classes.

From *The Crusader* 2 (August 1920), 9. Reprinted by permission of Garland Publishing Co., New York, New York.

The Brazilian Government reimburses the immigrant for all reasonable expenses, including passage from any European or American port to a Brazilian port. It also supplies him with farm land, and loans him the necessary tools; in fact, does everything possible to aid and encourage him in getting settled upon a promising basis.

There are always opportunities in Brazil for immigrants of agricultural training, experience or tendency. No matter how much glutted may be the labor market of the industrial centers there is always room and a welcome for the agriculturist. Brazil, with a territory as large as that of the United States, without Alaska, does not yet come near to growing enough food products for her own people, but has to import large supplies from Chile and Argentina.

While Portuguese is the official language of the country, English is widely spoken, especially in the coast districts and the environs of the big cities.

Race snobbery and prejudice are unknown in Brazil. The country has had many high officials, including even the Chief Executive, who were patently of Negro blood. The Brazilian navy and army are largely composed of Negroes. All the big dreadnaughts have Negro crews. It is the land of opportunity par excellence for the Negro at this time. It is also the land of the future. Scientists have estimated that the Amazon Valley alone could support a population of over four hundred million. At present the population of Brazil is around twenty-four million, one-third of whom are of Negro blood, less than one-third white or nearwhite, and the rest of the population of Indian blood.

At present Brazil is the greatest coffee and rubber country in the world. (In time it will supplant the United States as the greatest cotton growing and agricultural country in the world.) Its valleys and plateaus offer unlimited opportunities for agriculture, stock-raising, dairy farming, cotton growing and numerous other fields in which the United States, Canada, Australia and New Zealand at present lead the world. It is admirably served by the greatest river system in the world, ably seconded by a rapidly expanding railway system, and offers countless opportunities to the industrious for the accumulation of wealth and the "pursuit of happiness" unhampered by the man-hunt and the segregation law.

7.

[Associated Negro Press], "Wonderful Opportunities Offered in Brazil for Thrifty People of All Races"

CHICAGO, DEC. 10—Because of the widespread interest in the possibilities of living in South America, the Associated Negro Press has held a series of interviews with George Rambo, a man of our group, who has recently returned from that continent, with amazing stories of what Colored people may accomplish.

"Early in the summer of 1920," says Mr. Rambo, "in company with two Chicago and one West Virginia gentlemen, I made a trip from New York to Rio de Janeiro, on one of the English ships plying between these cities. We had heard many wonderful stories of the greatness of that country. But nothing we had heard, it developed, were equal to things we saw.

"Brazil is a republic, the constitution and law making bodies being very similar to those of the United States. A law abiding foreigner has the same privilege and is given the same protection that are given natives, except the right to vote. Voting can be acquired after a residence of two years in the republic.

"Brazilians, without regard to race or color, are as

From the *Tulsa Star*, December 11, 1920.

one big family, standing together on grounds of absolute equality or opportunity. There are no distinctions whatever, other than those imposed by wealth, culture and position. . . .

"We saw foreign people from the Mediterranean countries of Europe, who have been there only a year, joining with the native born in celebration of the numerous holidays. And why shouldn't they? I know of no place in the world where the conditions are more favorable to peace and comfort to the ordinary person than in this country. It is possible to live with very little effort in that land of abundance. But I do not say this as an inducement for the lazy and shiftless. In a cold country nature provides grudgingly, but in Brazil everything grows in great abundance. The streams are full of fish; the air is filled with birds; rich fruit, nuts, and herbs are gathered almost everywhere any day of the year. Two and three crops are harvested. Since no coal and few clothes are needed for warmth, it is no wonder that the oppressed and half starved of other lands find reasons for rejoicing.

"The Brazilian is always kind and courteous, and I was especially pleased to note the beauty of the family life. As a father and husband the Brazilian man has few equals. Divorces are practically unknown, and the grownup married children generally live with the parents. I have seen families with forty members, parents, children and grandchildren. The Brazilians rule their families with love rather than the rod.

"I think the courts are fair, and if anything, inclined to leniency. I saw only one man arrested, and that for intoxication—within two hours the same man passed me in the street smiling.

"Even slavery was never cruel and harsh in Brazil. The

relation of slave to master was much in the nature of a hired servant. They belonged to the same church, observed the same feast days, and often married into the family of the master. Today the same fraternal relationship exists. All celebrate Emancipation day together. It is a national holiday like our Fourth of July.

"The country is fortunate in having no deep national wounds to heal. There is no division of the country caused by difference of opinion on the slave question. Thirty-two years ago the slaves were freed by universal common consent without shedding a drop of blood. Brazil, it will be remembered, secured independence from Portugal without bloodshed. Such a country and such people have a great future.

"American Colored people are invited to participate in the upbuilding of a great nation in Brazil. I hope my people in this country will see the wonderful opportunities offered them. Read books and study maps concerning the country. It is not advisable for people to go there for location without becoming land owners, unless equipped for work of a high technical character.

"Expert accountants, stenographers, scientists in medicine, dentistry and engineering are in demand. As all new countries, Brazil is largely an agricultural and mining country. Employment in the cities is not so easily obtained. Brazil wants people to settle in the country districts. There has been organized a syndicate composed of prominent Brazilians and American Colored men to point the way for those who wish to pioneer. The syndicate has a capital of $500,000 with offices in Chicago and Rio de Janeiro. It is called the Brazilian American Colonization Syndicate. Land of excellent quality, well timbered, good water can be bought at about four dollars an acre in 250 acre tracts. Corn, beans, rice and all root crops yield at least two crops a year. South America, it seems to me, has greater possibilities than Africa."

8.
L. H. Stinson, "South America and Its Prospects in 1920"

> *L. H. Stinson, a physician from Augusta, Georgia, was one of sixteen African Americans who went to Brazil in the summer of 1920 to explore possibilities for the Negro there.*

ON AUGUST 1, 1920 a party (or our party) arrived in Rio de Janeiro, Brazil. Passing up the channel we beheld the most beautiful scenery and certainly one of the most beautiful harbors in the world. On either side of the channel we could see mountains with their green fruit trees of all descriptions, tall palms, and giant oaks. Here and there a mountain hut covered with bamboo or gutta percha. In the valleys were fertile fields, prairies, grasses and healthy cattle, grazing or basking in the tropical morning sun, just peeping from the clouds. Further in the bay we saw a beautiful little island, upon which was situated a light house, here and there were ships and motor boats plowing up and down the bay and we could see the South Americans, dressed in their light and palm beach

From the *Atlanta Independent*, December 23, 1920.

clothes and bamboo hats, dotting from place to place on the ships. In short, everything seemed to be as beautiful as nature could make it, and life seemed to be everlasting happiness. . . .

. . . We were surprised to find that the South Americans were so mixed as to race. There is absolutely no color line. The native Brazilians are mixed Spanish, Portuguese, and Indians. Therefore some are dark, some bright and some very fair, yet they all have beautiful hair. They termed us Americans from the North and never once referred to us as Negroes. We stayed at hotels where we pleased, mixed with all classes and color of people. Their churches are Catholic, all attend the same churches and schools. The government officials, street car motormen and conductors and police officials are all mixed. It was a common sight to see bright and dark children being led by the same parents, they being the same color as the children. . . .

The higher class Brazilian is very desirous of colored North Americans settling in Brazil. They look upon the North American Negro as being far advanced in civilization and intelligence; hence they believe that his citizenship would be an asset to their country. On the other hand, they are not desirous of white immigration because they believe they would try to consume all of their resources and control the country. The government offers every inducement to immigrants desiring to settle in Brazil. If one desires to venture out in agriculture or cattle raising, the government will furnish the land and implements for same; transportation from any part of the country, to [the] place desired for settlement, under an agreement that payment begins three years from date of contract, at which time settlers have the option of buying the land or paying a yearly per cent of profit made.

They prefer groups of five to ten each constituting a family. When requested your steamer will be refunded. A person, seven persons [*sic*] with some capital could invest in any business and especially exports and in a few years accumulate a fortune. Since the war the Germans are flocking there in large numbers but are in a colony to themselves.

So the Negro needs to wake up and get busy, while the Golden Harvest is yet in its embryonic stage.

9.
E. R. James, "Brazil as I Found It"

> E. R. James was a stockholder in the Attucks Realty Company of Seattle, Washington. He spent several months in Brazil in 1920 and 1921 and prepared a three-part report for the Chicago Defender, *published on May 28, June 4, and June 11, 1921.*

... THERE ARE opportunities in Brazil in plenty and for all men alike regardless of race, creed or color. But let us not mislead any one by making this statement wholly without qualifications. When I say opportunities in plenty, I mean opportunities for men trained in professions, trades and business men with some capital who are willing to go on the land and make sacrifices until such time as they have gotten a start.

For an ordinary laborer or men looking for ordinary positions, such as clerkships, hotel work, post office work, etc., Brazil is not the place. . . . Brazil is overrun with cheap European labor and the average wage paid for that class of work is so low that a North American could not exist on

From the *Chicago Defender*, June 4, 1921. Reprinted by permission of the *Chicago Daily Defender*.

it, and yet, I say, there are plenty of opportunities in Brazil for the right kind of men. High class engineers, electrical, civil or mechanical, are in good demand and command very good salaries. There are also openings for good business men who can take charge of manufactories, large stores, shipping houses, etc., and men of this caliber receive very good salaries, indeed, in many instances $5,000 and $10,000 per year and in one particular instance I was told of an English firm that pays its manager $22,000 per year. This means great opportunity for our trained young men, for we must always keep in mind one fact, that race or color prevents no man from getting a position in Brazil. The blackest man in America can get the best position in Brazil if he is qualified, and can retain it if he has the ability. But the opportunities do not cease with positions. There are many fine opportunities and openings in business for men with some capital and business experience, the most noticeable of these, to me, being the mercantile business, the real estate business and the express or delivery business. Most all of the goods sold by the retail stores in the city of Rio are delivered by men carrying on their heads such things as beds, bed springs, mattresses, wardrobes, trunks and all kinds of vegetables and foodstuffs. . . .

And now let us give a little space to the social conditions in Brazil. If I were asked the question, "Are there race prejudices in Brazil?" I would answer both in the affirmative and in the negative—yes, as far as the American people are concerned, and NO, a thousand times, as far as the Brazilian people are concerned. During our brief stay of three months in Brazil we had several instances brought to our notice which gave conclusive proof of the intention of the American people to carry their race prejudices with them into whatever country they go, as far as it is possible to do so. On the other hand, I did my best to find some trace of prejudice among the Brazilian people, kept my eyes and ears open for it and went out of my way to look for it. But I failed to find it. It is not there. It is not there socially, it is not there economically, it is not there politically. It is not there at all.

I made it my especial business to visit the different government departments, the railroad department, the land department, the post office department and the marine department and in every instance I found the people of color quite as well represented as the white people and in no instance is the slightest difference made between one and the other. Every man is given the position he is capable of filling, regardless of race or color. They have Colored captains and generals in their army and navy, they have had Colored presidents and they now have Colored senators and governors.

In private life and business the same good feeling prevails. In most any of the large stores, shipping offices and other places of business one can see whites and blacks peacefully and harmoniously working together, while on the streets, in the theaters, in the hotels and cafés people seem to mix and associate indiscriminately, apparently blind to the fact that some are one color and some another. On the street cars of the city Colored motormen with white conductors or white motormen with Colored conductors are commonly seen working together, while on all the railroads of the country Colored engineers, firemen and conductors are freely employed.

Intermarriage of the races is not only not prohibited but encouraged in Brazil, the idea of the people being to completely assimilate the dark races in time, and by a chart showing the rate of assimilation during the past twenty years they show that this idea can be accomplished within seventy-five to one hundred years.

In short, the Brazilian people are not possessed with the insane idea that the world was intended for the white man alone and that the white man is the only man who has virtues worthy of assimilation and consideration.

Yes, my readers, freedom and justice and liberty are to be had in Brazil, and nowhere in the whole wide world to my knowledge can a man of color enjoy those God given rights and privileges as fully and freely as in that country. And let us be thankful to Providence that there is one great country to the south of us, with resources calculated to be sufficient to support nearly half the people of the whole world, to which we can send our children as things grow blacker and blacker, harder and harder here in this country, knowing that they will be permitted to make use of their educations and talents, that they will be permitted to grow, to expand, to reach out to the fullest extent of their ability to become men and women.

10.

Frank St. Claire, "Sidelights on Brazil Racial Conditions"

Frank St. Claire frequently wrote for The Negro World, *the newspaper of Marcus Garvey and the Universal Negro Improvement Association.*

IN BRAZIL you will find Negroes in every walk of life. . . . While on a visit in Brazil I found the editor and proprietor of the leading daily paper of Rio de Janeiro was a Negro. I was introduced to the Archbishop of Amazonas, whose face was as black as any African Negro's. There are colored men and women at nearly every hotel table, and in the dining rooms on the steamers there are as many colored people at the tables as whites. . . .

Economic Advantages

Brazil offers many good opportunities for farmers and people of professions and trades. Persons with trades can earn the same amount of money in Brazil as in the United States. In Brazil it is your ability, knowledge and character

From *The Negro World* (New York City), January 13, 1923.

that count, and what you make of yourself, not your color or where you were born. It is not advisable for anyone from North America to go to Brazil to work as an ordinary laborer—far from it. The reason why West Indians succeed is because the living conditions in the West Indies are similar to those of Southern Europe. You will find the Brazilian Negro is not found wanting in commercial enterprise, excluding that which is owned by foreigners, mostly Germans, Japanese and Frenchmen. Many of the largest firms in Brazil are owned and controlled by colored Brazilians. Not only that but they do not do business on racial lines. Any line of business that pays in the United States will pay in Brazil, especially steam laundries, express wagons and the moving van business. . . .

Racial Characteristics

In character the Brazilian Negroes differ entirely from Negroes in Anglo-Saxon countries, and are also far different from the peasants of Europe. They can be led but not driven. They are not of a servile or submissive disposition. They also have a powerful sense of mother wit. They are quite similar to the Irish in this respect, except that they are not quite so full of humor, and at a weak moment are likely to commit suicide.

In the large cities they differ greatly from those of the rural districts and small towns. During a hard struggle for livelihood you find them sullen, silent and sensitive, but agreeable. Their emotions arise entirely from political conditions. In religion they are tolerant Catholics, but 75 per cent of the men do not attend any church. You seldom hear them discuss religion. Colored priests, bishops and archbishops preside over mixed congregations. A large number of them are freethinkers. Suicide among the Brazilian Negroes is nothing new, according to Fletcher and Kidder's "Brazil and the Brazilians." It was a common occurrence among Negro slaves, yet slavery was not near as harsh, as far as the Latins were concerned, as it was in the English speaking countries. Large numbers of slaves bought their freedom and became educated and wealthy. Slaves often helped to buy the freedom of others. One good point about the Brazilian Negro is that he is not jealous of another person's success. Another point is that he is self-reliant, proud but polite. While he is firm and somewhat unsympathetic, he is humane and considerate of both natives and foreigners. He is not prejudiced as to color. He hates the North American white man on account of his attitude toward darker races. They refer to them as gringos. During the late war the Germans played on this sentiment to their advantage, as Northern Brazil was strongly pro-German. . . .

The reason why they object to being called Negroes is on account of the way the word is used in Anglo-Saxon countries—not because they are ashamed—far from it. In the churches you will find images of all shades and colors corresponding with the people of the country.

General Conditions, Past and Present

In writing of social life in Brazil, so far as the big four hundred is concerned, many North American and English writers say Negroes are barred on account of race. Not so—the big four hundred of Brazil are similar to the French nobility. They do not admit Germans, Italians or anyone else. They are very exclusive. They are permitted to hold their titles. They were formerly connected with the household of Dom Pedro II, last Emperor of Brazil. Next to them comes the gentry class, made up of wealthy Brazilians—colored, Germans, Jews, Italians, French and Portuguese—who worked up to that class. Race or color has nothing to do with the matter. Many so-called educated Negroes in the United States think in the western world Negroes are only in English speaking countries. If a person comes from one of the Latin countries, even if he has Negro features, if he or she speaks another language, shows courage, is well educated and a Catholic, the people don't think of him as colored, because their minds have not been enslaved by Anglo-Saxon psychology in regard to race.

11.
Robert S. Abbott, "My Trip Through South America"

> Robert S. Abbott (1868–1940) was born of former slave parents in Georgia and educated at Hampton Institute, Virginia, where he learned the printer's trade, and at Kent College of Law in Chicago. After practicing law briefly in Topeka, Kansas; Gary, Indiana; and Chicago, in 1905 he founded the Chicago Defender. Within a decade it grew from a four-page paper of handbill size to one of the leading African-American newspapers, and Abbott became wealthy enough to undertake a three-month trip to South America in 1923. Upon his return he wrote a series of lengthy articles for the Defender, which are excerpted here. For details on his trip and experiences in Brazil, see the biography of Abbott by Roi Ottley, The Lonely Warrior: The Life and Times of Robert S. Abbott (Chicago, 1955), 228–46; and David J. Hellwig, "A New Frontier in a Racial Paradise: Robert S. Abbott's Brazilian Dream," Luso-Brazilian Review 25 (Summer 1988), 59–67.

This series of articles originally appeared in the Chicago Defender, August 4 to October 27, 1923. Reprinted by permission of the Chicago Daily Defender.

Article 1: "Personal Motives," Part One (August 4, 1923)

It was with secret thrills of a peculiar and inexpressible joy that I, at last, on the third day of last February, accompanied by my wife, sailed from the port of New York for a visit to the South American republics. It was the opening chapter in realization of a golden dream long cherished. Time after time had I made plans for such a trip, but ever and anon some exigency of business had arisen....

My desire to visit South America was actuated primarily by the further desire to observe the social pulse of the Negro placed in a climatic environment similar to that of his original African home, and one in which life was stimulated by the exigencies of modern society; to ascertain the nature of the Negro's social progress when projected within the sphere of a Latin-European tradition and culture, of which I had reason to believe to be wholly devoid of those singularly irrational social-mental attitudes, based on a consciousness of race differences—that which has been so strangely potent in hindering the natural and wholesome evolution of 12 millions of Negroes within the confines of North American society; more, to grasp somehow, however superficial, the major lines of South American ethnic evolution, as thus probably indicative of what might be her future ethnic homogeneity; and further, to not only comprehend the real status of the Negro in South American society, but to ferret out in a broad sense the possible industrial, commercial and social opportunities for that enlightened and growing group of North American Negroes, who so recently are beginning to look to the South American continent as, after all, the most likely haven for a solution of their individual problems.

Some Unexpected Opposition

But in the very first stage of preparation for the voyage we were confronted with a set of irritating circumstances of which I shall not herein fail to mention: We applied to the Lamport & Holt Steamship company for sailing accommodations, and after some delay were informed that all first class accommodations had been taken—this, it seems—and we have all reasons to believe—was nothing more than an act of racial discrimination. To prove that this was race discrimination my wife[1] called at the office and she was offered a ticket (first class) on the boat that refused me passage.

And the flagrant act of racial discrimination we suffered in the offices of the above named company is by no means a distinction of that company. For we immediately found from that moment what seems to be a general agreement or common understanding among all the steamship offices located in Chicago against selling first class passage to Negroes. We went hither and thither, calling at all the steamship offices, and the only varying features identical with their respective policies of denying Negroes first class accommodation were the degrees of discomfiture to which we were put. It was only after fully two months of constant effort that we succeeded. . . .

Then came the business of securing passport visas from the respective consuls stationed at Chicago, representing the several South American countries we had proposed to visit. When called upon each and all rendered me the most prompt and cordial service—all save the consul from Brazil. His was a flat refusal, and that solely on the ground of being Negroes. This, no doubt, may strike the reader as strangely interesting, considering the fact that the republic of Brazil has a Negro population far exceeding in relative proportion that which obtains between Negroes and whites in the United States of North America.

I at once called the attention of Congressman Martin B. Madden to the circumstance, requesting him to lend his efforts. This he did, but seemed quite unable to accomplish anything. . . .

I then turned to Senator Medill McCormick. Forthwith the matter was taken up with the Brazilian embassy. It was only after much effort and refined judgment on the part of Senator Medill McCormick was there anything achieved on this score. . . .

Thus it was only after pressure was brought to bear did I succeed in getting the consul from Brazil to visa our passports. This, it seems, has been the experience of every American Negro during the last few years who has sought entry into Brazil. But why is such the case?

Barrier Broken

We later discovered that the conduct of these Brazilian consuls, stationed in several American cities, in refusing to visa anyone's passport on the ground of race is entirely contrary to the Brazilian national constitution and shamefully at variance with the finely democratic temper of the Brazilian people.

Could this circumstance be in any way a lingering feature of some secret prohibitive policy against Negro emigration inaugurated under the Wilson administration?

Then it was that the Negro for the first time on his own initiative made it quite plain how indispensable he is to American industry. One might have been willing to believe that at some recent time a gentlemen's agreement had been effected with the Brazilian government to help to keep American Negro labor at home, and without, at the same time, making a formal distinction between the worker and the tourist. But such has not been the case. Brazil needs people. With an expanse of territory something larger than that of the United States of North America, leaving out Alaska, but possessing a population of only about twenty-four million, it is imperative that she encourage immigration; and this she has done and is doing at a cost of millions of milreis. To her shores gather in immigration representatives of every black, brown, yellow and white race under the sun.

And yet why Brazilian consuls in America are refusing to visa the passports of American Negroes remains an unanswered problem; but suffice it to say that such is wholly contradictory to a most rigid and well established constitutional law of Brazil.

Article 2: "Personal Motives," Part Two (August 11, 1923)

On February 15 we entered the bewitching Bay of Rio. It was triumphal. This bay is like an inland sea; encircled by high, bristling mountains appearing like titanic giants in battle array. The grim immensity of background is relieved only by the soft, sunny shores, the superabundance of varicolored flowers and mysterious islands here and there nestled like great emeralds in the calm, iridescent waters of the bay. The dazzling lights of the sky and the waters blend in subtle, sensuous effect. We catch sight of the city—Rio de Janeiro, or January River, so called by the first comers from Portugal, in the year 1500, who took the bay for a river. And the city, against its background of huge, swelling green hills, and reflecting resplendent spots, appears as a rare phenomenon. The distance is wreathed with a soft light haze that slowly dissolves as our approach nears the quay.

Having come ashore, we now take route through Avenida Central, a magnificent highway that would be the pride of any capital city in the world. The motor car sped swiftly, and now at high level above the bay and most of the city we got a finely attractive view of the latter. Embraced on the one side by the softly purling waters, on the other by the ever-encroaching tropical forest. In this part of the world the force of nature is irresistible. Man must put forth prodigious effort to protect himself from the very fertility and productiveness of the soil. Below, the city, in marvelous, majestic beauty, spreads out to the bay.

American Color-Prejudice

We move on. Our objective is the Gloria hotel, a first-class American establishment. One might wonder why we had elected to stop at an American hotel, knowing as we did the established custom in North America of denying Negroes this civil privilege. But many of the American acquaintances we made during the voyage had insisted that we put up at the Gloria hotel; that they were going to stop there and that aside from the high quality of its service, English was almost the sole language spoken there, and thus we would be relieved to a large degree of a common difficulty one meets when traveling in a foreign country. We arrive at the Gloria hotel. But behold! even here we are met by that incubus monster who, like a legendary sea serpent, it seems, has trailed our course down the South Atlantic way and proposes to find an abode in Brazil. It is American Color-Prejudice. Even in the fair land of Brazil, whose heart pulses, whose every fiber is vibrant with the democratic traditions of the great French revolution, the slimy thing of American colorphobia would presume to assert itself. We were politely told there were no vacancies. But we knew differently. Leaving, we went to the Hotel Victoria, a first-class Brazilian establishment, where accommodations were unhesitatingly and even graciously extended us.

The population of Rio de Janeiro is estimated at 1,175,000. A very large part of this number are Negroes, both of mixed and pure blood. It is very difficult for a native even to say just what the Negro population is in any city or part of the Republic, as census is not based on any group distinctions. The cosmopolitanism of Rio de Janeiro is evident on every hand; men and women of all complexions and intermedial shades commingle and move freely in the daily currents of full, active life. This was impressive! And as a Negro and a product of American traditions, my natural, logical reaction was the desire to reach some clear, positive conclusion as to the real depth and extent of this Brazilian democratic spirit, or to what degree it was truly inclusive of the Negro. And this, I feel that I have done.

Some Meetings

The proprietor and other officials of the Hotel Victoria at once set out with special efforts to help to make our sojourn in Rio de Janeiro a happy one. And in a very short time we were afforded the pleasure of making the acquaintance of many persons of distinction, eminent in the affairs of commerce, government, the liberal professions, etc. And not only were we given to know these personages in their broader social contact, but with a grace unmistakably sincere were accorded the most cordial reception at their homes and tables. And I cannot help feel that among many of the acquaintances made in that fair city below the equator, there will ripen the deepest friendships, and that no doubt out of the mobility, the grand democratic fullness of their hearts, there shall emanate an altruism to create a better understanding of the North American Negro and his problems.

At once we were given formal introduction to an unusually interesting figure in the person of Dr. Alfredo Clendenden. He is a North American Negro by birth, but went from New York to Brazil more than forty years ago. He studied dentistry, entered upon his profession, and before long became dentist to the emperor, Dom Pedro II, who was yet on the Brazilian throne at that time. Today he is an appointed dentist to the Rio de Janeiro Opera; active in a number of public affairs and quite a distinguished and well known figure in the society of the capital. And in spite of his seventy years of age is as vigorous and vivacious as a man of thirty. It was through Dr. Alfredo Clendenden that we were given the pleasure of meeting some of the most eminent persons of the Brazilian capital. To mention some few:

José do Patrocinio, Jr., is a very eminent journalist and until quite recently secretary of the Brazilian embassy at Brussels, Belgium. He is a son of a very distinguished figure in recent Brazilian history, also of whom I shall have occasion to mention later. Senhor Patrocinio, Jr., is much of a favorite throughout polite society of the capital.

Juliano Moreira is a doctor of medicine from the High School of Medicine of Bahia. He is considered one of the most illustrious of physicians and neurologists in the republic. He was appointed by the government to represent Brazil at the International Congress of Neurologists held at Berlin, and for twenty years has been director of the National hospital and a professor of psychiatry.

Senhor Eloy de Souza is a senator of the republic, and for twenty years or more has enjoyed constant re-election. At the same time he is quite eminent as a writer and journalist.

Senhor Sampaio Correia is also a senator of the republic, chief of the political party known as "Alliansa Republicano," and at the same time a professor in the High School of Engineering. In the last election he had a plurality of 10,000 votes over his white opponent.

Senhor Tito Carlos is quite a young man, born in the city of Parahyba [Paraiba] in 1900. He was at one time staff member of the "Renascensa" of that city; having recently made his residence in Rio de Janeiro he is acquiring fame as a writer and journalist. Further, in 1924, he is to take his degree in medicine from the National University of Rio de Janeiro.

Senhor Evaristo de Moraes is regarded as one of the greatest of Brazilian criminologists; a famed lawyer and orator. He is a graduate of the High School of Law of Rio de Janeiro.

Captain Iguacio C. Villarinho is a distinguished officer in the federal army of the republic.

... Dr. Olympio de Castro, a priest, and a man of great scholarly attainments.

It is not by chance that those whom I have above mentioned are Negroes, Negroes in a close meaning of that term; it is that I wished at the same time to show the height to which the individual Negro can rise through sheer ability when allowed the social opportunities. Too, I experienced pleasant astonishment in perceiving the nimble grasp a few of those personages had on the Negro problem in North America. There is no kind of race problem in Brazil, but the love of liberty is so deeply engraved in the Brazilian soul that there is no measure of effort on the part of many Brazilian leaders to understand the social sufferings of any section of oppressed humanity.

Article 3: "São Paulo" (August 18, 1923)

Again American Color Prejudice

We arrived in São Paulo in the late afternoon. We went to the Palace hotel, were assigned accommodations, but, irritating as it may seem, during the night we were quietly informed by the proprietor that there were quite a number of American tourists, guests in the hotel, who objected to our presence, and asked that we give up our suite. The hour was late and I positively refused. The next morning I went to the Odeste hotel. Nevertheless there are thousands of Negroes in São Paulo, and we found their social status about the same as those of Rio de Janeiro. We had the pleasure of meeting Senhor T. D. de Castro, a Negro, minister of the interior of the state of São Paulo. We accepted an invitation to tea at his home. Senhor de Castro is an ardent admirer of the late Dr. Booker T. Washington, and named his son Booker T. Washington de Castro in honor of him. This de Castro family we found in every respect quite typical of the new aristocracy to which the republic of recent years has given birth; an aristocracy founded, not as in the days of the empire on blood or birth, but on true culture, patriotic usefulness and high moral principle.

The Melting Pot of Races

A very interesting ethnological map of Brazil might be drawn. Slavery tailed off in the southern areas, never penetrating the most southern states. Today in the latter the population is almost wholly German, Italian, Russian, the principal races of Europe and a few Japanese colonies. In the central sections of the republic the people are largely of the mestizo type—that is, an intermixture of Indian and Portuguese white. Moving north the types darken; slowly the African blood becomes dominant. And when one has reached the states in which are located the cities of Bahia and Pernambuco, the pure African is the common and characteristic type. Going still further north the Negro and white fade out and the Indian becomes the dominant type. Upon this great mixed blood mass the educational system of the republic and the Latin idea are effectively making their way.

Almost every race under the sun is found in Brazilian society, and there is a daily increase through a perpetual stream of immigration. But in spite of the great variety and broad differences of physical type and mental outlook, there is a state of absolute social harmony. Negroes and whites intermarry without provoking the slightest social criticism. Further, the tendency seems to encourage intermarriage between widely different stocks, such as white and African—the ideal being a perfect political state thoroughly homogeneous in blood.

There is a peculiar something in the temperament of the Portuguese much akin to the same something in the Frenchman that enables him to get along quite well with the darker races. The warm, sympathetic, imaginative nature of the Portuguese seems to find its counterpart in the Negro. A brilliant future is assured for the section of the Negro Race in Brazil, and out of the milieu of racial crossings in that country shall come a people for [sic] physical beauty, intelligence, vigor and progressive instinct without peer anywhere in the world. . . .

Article 4: "Rio de Janeiro," Part Two (September 1, 1923)

Industrial Opportunities

The North American Negro proposing to settle in Brazil should have either one of two things: Some money or a trade or profession. As yet corporative business in Brazil has not developed to the point it has in this country, wherein the business man of small means finds it almost impossible to expand. Commerce in Brazil is still in the competitive stage and a fair field of activity is limitless for the individual business man of ambition and energy. As yet there are no syndicates, trusts or monopolies in the country to crush or destroy the business efforts of the individual. Therefore it requires by no means the amount of capital to enter business in Brazil that it does in North America.

Again, the man or woman who can do things never

suffers the slightest handicap because of race. The trades and professions are thrown open to all persons regardless of race or color, and employment or a clientele is assured solely on the consideration of one's merit. . . .

Too, there is the abundant productivity of the soil that enables the cultivator to get two and three crops a year. Sugar cane, cocoa, coffee, tobacco, rubber and cotton are some of the chief staples of the country. The many of our Race in the Southern states who have become experts in the production of sugar cane, tobacco and cotton would find numerous advantages much above any they may now enjoy in the cultivation of these same staples in Brazil. More than the superior soil and climate for the farmer, there is liberty and a decent compensation for one's products. . . .

Americans in Brazil

The North American Negro in seeking knowledge on life in Brazil invariably turns to the more ready sources of books of travel, written by Englishmen or Americans, lectures and film pictures. But at each turn in seeking information particularly pertaining to his own Race in Brazil he is always disappointed. It was this that lent much to my desire to visit Brazil, and to allay once for all times the agitating eagerness I suffered to know something of the life and conditions of that second major section of the Race in the new world. It now appears, and quite conclusive, that there is a conscious, deliberate, even though tacit, effort on the part of the Englishman or American to leave out whenever possible any reference or exhibition of Negro life in treating of Brazil. One might be willing to believe that the American's sense of patriotism forbids his disclosing to any section of the American public the fact that social equality can exist for the Negro anywhere in the world....

There is a rapidly awakening interest among white Americans toward Brazil and the great and numerous opportunities she proffers the man of ambition and energy. And some white Americans have settled in Brazil, and even from our southern states. If this latter type suffered any discomfiture from the presence of the Negro before leaving, they have but rendered it infinitely more in removing their residence to Brazil. For there Negro people are evident on every hand, enjoying with inconceivable ease the entire facilities of a present-day democracy. And yet too often the American does when possible attempt to establish his time-honored custom of race discrimination. The Brazilian, who is quite unfamiliar with these sort of practices, is naturally slow in understanding them as such. And therein lies a weakness. The Brazilian is of an inherent, instinctive democratic spirit, and quite unable to understand otherwise in others. He had rather feel that a victim of race discrimination had made a mistake in interpreting the act as such than otherwise. Particularly in matters like this, to the Negro from North America, the Brazilian seems a bit too sentimental....

Yet the Brazilian Negro, once he becomes convinced that he is being made to suffer because of his race, becomes aroused to a most bitter pitch of resentment. As an example: There was a certain white Brazilian professor, a member of one of Brazil's leading universities, who had been educated in the United States. This man, through years of contact in this country, had also imbibed some portion of American race-prejudice. One day it came about that he found occasion to insult, in regard his race, a Negro student and member of his class; and this he did by drawing a small mirror from his pocket, thrusting it before the student's face and saying: "Look at yourself, I have been educated in North America and I don't have to teach your kind." Overwhelmed with vicious anger the student, the following day, came to the classroom armed and shot the former to death in the midst of his class. . . .

Article 4 (continued): "Rio de Janeiro," Part Three (September 8, 1923)

It was the spirit of adventure stirring in the bosoms of a few individuals of the early sixteenth century that disclosed to Europe and to the world the existence of new continents on this side of the Atlantic. And altogether it has been those races who were full of the spirit of adventure and the courage to dare to branch out into new areas of the globe and build up new communities suitable to new ideals of social freedom. The early settlers of the American continents were sorely dissatisfied with the narrow, oppressed life of Europe, and with sublime faith in their own inherent powers, threw in their lot with the unknown conditions of a new world. They were an admirable people, full of courage and the love of human dignity. The mind of a high quality, when finding itself in an unfavorable environment, does one of two things: Either it tries to modify the conditions about it, suitable to its liking, or it completely lifts itself out of the unfavorable environment. No progressive spirit would care to live in an age in which there were no agitators, nor can really thoughtful persons impeach a man for emigrating. When so doing the latter feels that he is bettering his social condition. The great empire-building races of the earth have been those in which there were countless elements, who not only craved the highest possible social freedom, but who at the same time had the daring to go out and seek it, come what may. Liberty and the opportunities of self-expression are the highest, noblest aims any man can have. And is it not the degree in which this condition is vouchsafed each and every member of a given society by which we adjudge the civilization of that society? Wealth is not civilization; nor is it ever an end within itself. It is a means to an end; and that end is the ideal condition in which there may be the highest degree of individual liberty consistent with the commonweal.

Beginning of Great American Fortunes

The great industrial wealth that we see about us was not built up solely as the outcome of individual ideas. It is the acme of a long period of growth, dating back to the time when land everywhere was incredibly cheap, when the government gave land concessions to railroad and mining companies and subsidies, to even encourage and stimulate the expansion of our economic life. The foundations of great American fortunes were laid when the Negro was yet a slave and could not have gotten in on the ground floor and grown up as an integral and organic part of the industrial fibre.

The marvelous and rich railroads, steamships, factories, mines, mills, etc., are not the corporated investments of wage-earners, but the merger of countless small enterprises beginning immediately after the Civil War. This is the day of big or corporative business in American life. And the individual enterprise of small capital only succeeds where it does not suffer competitive conflict with the big corporations.

South and Progress

The American economic structure was pretty well established when the slaves were emancipated. But excluding this fact, the Negro in America has by no means had a fair chance to show his higher inherent worth to social progress. Conditions in the South keep him forever on the defensive. His best energies are directed not toward the development of permanent and worth-while enterprises, but to organized efforts to maintain his social being.

It is beyond estimation as to what would have and could be the achievements of the Negro in America if he were not constantly harassed by lynching, discrimination, disfranchisement and the maltreatment of his women. And how can a people rise borne down with these social abuses, not only to a plane of economic independence, but to the full height of manly courage, morality and intelligence.

Progress in the South is necessarily slow, and that because the white South refuses to be civilized; it refuses to recognize the sociological fact that social progress is ever determinable on ever increasing cooperation among the elements that constitute society.

Brazil and Negro Opportunities

Slavery was abolished in Brazil only as late as 1888. Yet the Negro's importance in the political and intellectual life of Brazil far transcends that of the Negro in North America. And this because there have been no obstacles put athwart his path of free development. To estimate the Negro's advancement in Brazil is not to name individuals of the Race who stand out with any degree of eminence in the various walks of life. It would be like measuring the Race's political position in North America in terms of individual Negro political appointees. It is the general average, the condition of the masses, that count most; their educational, economic and moral welfare. In North America the avenues of occupation open to the Negro are comparatively few. In Brazil it is altogether quite different. The trades, professions and business are freely open to any and every person. And one's progress therein depends not on traditions in respect to race or color, but sheer ability. The economic conditions of the plain people are conspicuously good. One evidencing feature is the tidy, clean appearance of the numerous children of all colors—black, white, brown and yellow—seen playing hither and thither in the parks, boulevards, thoroughfares and everywhere.

But common to all Latin-American countries, the immigrant into Brazil should have the knowledge of either a trade or profession, and if neither, then some bit of capital with which to go into business.

Military Strength

Many of the highest officers of both the army and navy are Negroes. But in very recent years there has developed a sentimental movement emanating from a certain white section of society to oppose the prepondering influence Negroes are acquiring in the navy.

These whites it seems are largely of the old aristocracy, originating in colonial days, who have always, even since the beginning of the republic, not only held themselves exclusively aloof, but have opposed latter day republican innovations. But this ancient aristocracy in Brazil is small and its days are few. Too, it seems that Americans have, to a large degree, been responsible for the more recent manifestation of the sentiment.

The average Negro of Brazil, when invited to give his opinion on the matter, expresses himself in very vehement terms and tells you that they, the Negro people of Brazil, through many years, have become familiar with seeing black commanders treading the admiral's bridge on Brazil's battleships, and that this must and ever shall continue to be.

Article 10: "Havana and Sailing North"
(October 20, 1923)

Some Reflections

For a Negro visiting South America it is certainly worth all the time and money entailed. It was a delight beyond words to have observed the social life of the Negro, say, in Brazil, where, untrammeled by any racial feeling, he is climbing higher and higher in the scale of achievement. Yet the emancipation of the Negro in Brazil only dates from 1888. One wonders, no doubt, how it can be that in a land where slavery is yet in the memory of most adults, society is free of any prejudice or rancor against the once enslaved Race. And this is true. The careful student of social science does not attempt to point out any one cause for a social phenomenon. And in this instance there are a number of elements that enter into the fact of there being perfect equality between the races in Brazil. But certainly the following circumstances are among those most paramount in explaining the condition: The whites in Brazil are of the Latin race—Portuguese. And here it is a matter of temperament. Further, it was not the persistent growth of an industrial society that made the institution of slavery impossible within the same political system as with our North American republic. In Brazil it was the case of a highly sensitive moral nature worked up to a lofty sense of duty. The slave was freed without the slightest physical struggle and at once took his place as an equal in the life of the nation.

Here is a singular example of the influence of the social milieu on the mind: At one time during the course of the Civil War in North America a number of southern slave holders, fearing that the outcome of the struggle would be victory for the North, took their slaves and what other property they could and fled into Brazil, where, of course, slavery yet obtained. Settling in the interior they at once built up a community and named it Villa Americana—American Town. There they lived with their slaves on their new plantations for some years, until the time came for Brazil to emancipate her slaves. This was, of course, a much unexpected blow to Villa Americana. But today even in this town, slavery has left no social inconveniences for the Negro. More, the white sons and daughters of these former slave holders have intermarried and mixed freely with those who are the descendants of slaves.

Land of Opportunity

Brazil has a territory and natural resources able to sustain a population many times larger than that she now has. Definitely speaking, the hope of her future lies in encouraging immigration. And for one who has seen and gathered some positive and direct understanding of conditions for the North American Negro who would settle in Brazil, I would unhesitatingly say that for the Negro with a trade or profession, or who has some money and desires to go in business, Brazil offers unparalleled opportunities for life success. Again, in the state of Matto Grosso, Brazil, the climate and soil are finely adapted to cotton growing. The planter gets two crops a year, and a bale to the acre is common under the most ordinary circumstances. The state of Matto Grosso is very large in area, as large as our entire Southern states combined, but as yet quite sparsely settled. The Brazilian government is encouraging foreign immigration of the right type into Matto Grosso, and on excellent conditions. If one thousand of our agricultural families from the Southern states were to settle in Matto Grosso at this time and grow cotton I venture to say that with industry and clear-sightedness in a very few years they would become rich. In that state is found the best cotton growing land in the world, and procurable on very easy terms. And practically the same conditions hold for the state of Bahia.

Tobacco is also a staple of the country and is considered among the finest in the world. It has been largely left to nature until recent years, when some attention is now being given to its cultivation. I shall not attempt to enumerate even the most outstanding of Brazil's agricultural products, but suffice it to say that no country in the world is better adapted by reason of soil and climate to the growing of sugar cane, cotton, tobacco, rice, coffee, yerba matte and rubber plants. From a number of plants the farmer is able to get two and sometimes three crops a year.

Brazil is a new country, and as it has been throughout history, those who get in on the ground floor, as it were, enjoy the best opportunities for the accumulation of fortunes. We may see this in the economic history of our own United States. Those families today that are representatives of the great American fortunes are the direct descendants of the early American adventurers, men who were not afraid, and who dared to go out into new areas and build up an environment suitable to their own passions and philosophy of life.

The transportation system through the states of Matto Grosso and Bahia is not as developed as one would like, but improvements are constantly being made, and in 1925 the government is to build an admirable system of railroads connecting up those two states with the capital, Rio de Janeiro. That will be a great boon to those states—an increase in land values and a larger income to the agricultural producer. Already a white American company has acquired one million acres of land in the state of Matto Grosso. Let us not wait until the best in the way of land and opportunities have been appropriated by others before we attempt to acquire some advantages for ourselves.

At this point I may disclose the fact that plans are now being laid for organizing an excursion trip into South America of a party of three hundred or more Negro business and professional men for the year 1925. The vessel on which they are to sail will be chartered. The excursion will have the two-fold purpose of getting first hand information on opportunities in reference to commercial investment and at the same time to inculcate a better understanding among the South American people of the Negro of North America, and thus contribute much to offsetting the poisonous propaganda the white American is endeavoring to set afloat against the Negro in that continent. The party proposes to visit the great Negro city of Bahia in the state of that name; sail up the Amazon river for some distance in observation of the vast rubber growing territory; a visit to Pernambuco, the great coffee mart, and at the same time the second of Brazil's great Negro cities; a brief stay in the magnificent Brazilian capital, Rio de Janeiro, and ending with a trip to Buenos Aires to pay solemn tribute to the memory of General Filucho, the Negro martyr of Argentina political history.

This trip to South America will be promoted by Chicago Negro business men, together with men of the Race elsewhere noted for success and character. Their idea will be to open up a practical avenue for commercial enterprise and to create a connection in Brazil for the Negro of the United States who may desire to settle in a new country, under conditions more in harmony with his notion of freedom. Living in Brazil, considered in American money, is cheap, but comports with the high standard of modern civilization. Neither exploitation nor colonization is involved in this scheme of practical business.

These figures may interest the reader: In Brazil an eight-room house with a well and barn costs around $1,000, while one thousand acres of cultivable land may be bought for $1,000. Another $1,000 would furnish the house and clear the land.

In Brazil neither commercial nor social restrictions attach themselves to any man on account of race. Settlers in Brazil have no idea of taking the country, but are content to let the country take them. In Brazil all men are equal under the law and in society, and a man, white or black, may rise in soldiery, in state, in church and business as high as his brain and character will elevate him.

White Americans have entered into a contract with the Brazilian government to exploit a large section of the

Amazon river. As compensation they will build wharves and levees. This means that within a few years the rich interior of Brazil will have been reclaimed and civilization afforded a new stand. Side by side with the American white man, seeking an outlet for genius and money, should go the American Negro, bent upon a like mission.

No wholesale exodus of the American Negro is expected nor desired. The base of the future achievements of the Negro will remain, as now, in the United States.

No one race will ever again claim and people any one continent. Future nations will be erected on the experiences of the ages. Those experiences teach that claiming the soil in the name of a race is difficult to maintain and in the multitude of tongues and bloods civilization continues its sweep.

Brazil is a strong, liberty-loving nation, a country highly respected in the society of nations. There one may enjoy every comfort of modern progress and remain in touch with the active spirit of world thought. As other men have branched out into new worlds, under flags distant from the flag of their nativity, so must the American Negro, not upon the silly excursion of conquest, but as a practical idealist, determined to win his points in the fields and markets of the world by knowledge and industry.

"Brazil: The Land of Marvelous Opportunity" (October 27, 1923)

The world of today is activated by a fervid spirit of trade and finance, and such as never before. At no time in human history has the passion for money-making entered so largely into man's social fiber as now. Commerce is paramount, and all else is made to subserve. It is the underlying and motivating force of all modern progress. In promoting its interest new fields of research have been opened and great universal truths discovered in every ramification of human existence.

The United States of North America leads the world in wealth and commerce. And this she has been able to do, primarily, because of peculiar geographical conditions which made industry highly indispensable, the possession of extensive territory with abundant natural resources, and withal, in her early history the possession of a large slave population.

The foundation of our national economic system was laid long before the emancipation of the slave, and the latter could not have played any independent part therein. Back in those days land was cheap and the government did much to encourage industry. At the end of the colonial period our economic development became rapid, and with the close of the Civil War commences that peculiar and unexampled era in our business life: The birth of the corporation, trustification and the resultant monopolization of the sources of raw material. Today the pooling of large capital—big business—is the characteristic feature of our economic life.

Negro in Business

If today the Negro is a minor factor in American business life it is not attributable to lack of acumen, but rather to the fact that great corporations have acquired monopoly of the production of the necessaries of life, control their market, and are thus rapidly making in America individual enterprise a thing of the past. The man of small capital finds it increasingly harder to invest with profit, and more and more he is being forced into the working class.

In the Latin-American countries this crushing process of the centralization of national wealth in the hands of a few has not yet begun. There the man of small capital enjoys a limitless field for profitable investment without parallel anywhere in the world. These are facts which the Negro business man should well consider. But big capital, both British and American, is being steadily attracted into South America, and the North American Negro seeking economic advantages ought to clinch some of the present opportunities which that continent holds out to all persons, and particularly in the republic of Brazil.

Some Interesting Facts

Brazil has an immense territory, larger than the United States of North America if we omit Alaska. Its population numbers about 30 million, of which about half are Negroes, or of Negro extraction. But race identity has little bearing on the problems of life in Brazil. The fact that a man is black, yellow or white carries no social significance. Truly, it is a country where personal merit counts above all else! . . .

Negro Expansion

This is an age of expansion in which the more vigorous and ambitious types of mankind are refusing to be content to think in mere terms of race or nationality, but in terms of the world. Frenchmen, Germans, Englishmen, Italians, Japanese and white Americans may be found in every country of the globe; anywhere in which conditions are conducive to general personal well being.

There is no country in which the Negro is better placed than in Brazil, and which country will give to the Race a higher developed type of individual.

The above facts are of much significance and are entitled to the thoughtful consideration of those among us who are seeking fertile fields for investment, and others who desire better conditions for individual self-expression than our United States of North America has to offer.

NOTE

1. Abbott's wife, the former Helen Thornton Morrison, was a blue-eyed quadroon who was often mistaken for a white person.

12.

William Pickens, "Sightseeing in South America"

William Pickens (1881–1954) was an educator, orator, author, and civil rights leader. He was born in South Carolina and attended Talladega College and Yale University, where he completed a degree in classics in 1904. Subsequently he taught at Talladega, Wiley University in Marshall, Texas, and Morgan College in Baltimore. From 1920 to 1940 he worked for the NAACP national office in New York City as field secretary and director of branches.

WE WISH TO suggest some things which we hope the "official guides" in South America will not fail to point out to the North Americans who are to visit them in the entourage of Mr. Hoover.[1]

They need not point out any of their skyscrapers, for they have none that can vie with the Woolworth Building, nor any of their banks, for they cannot compete with Wall Street, nor any of their criminals, for they have none equal those of Chicago. Let them point out:

That in South America men of any race and color can hold any office they are able to hold.

From the *Philadelphia Tribune*, December 27, 1928.

That the absence of race discrimination in civil privileges have [sic] done no harm to anybody.

That children in public schools, without color lines, do not grow up into enmity but to friendship.

That lynching, which is one of the indispensable industries of Mississippi, is found to be absolutely needless in Brazil, which has cities with larger Negro populations than any city of Mississippi.

That race prejudice is not "natural and instinctive," but an abnormality and a misfit in civilization.

That Nordics, while they may be useful, are not at all necessary for the continued operation of the solar system.

You cannot astonish us materially, Miss South America; but show our skepticism some of the doubted wonders of your soul.

NOTE

1. Shortly after his election in the fall of 1928, President-elect Hoover took a ten-week "good will" tour of Latin America that included a stop in Brazil in late December.

PART II

The Myth Debated (1940-1965)

AFRICAN-AMERICAN interest in Brazil slackened considerably in the 1930s with the decline of nationalist movements in the United States and the struggle to survive the Great Depression. In the next decade, however, blacks paid much more attention to world affairs—and to Brazil. Enhanced opportunities for travel and education, a resurgence of protest during World War II as black Americans fought to achieve a victory for democracy at home as well as abroad, accelerated pressure by Africans and other colonized peoples for independence, and persistent reports of Brazilian opposition to African-American immigration served both to heighten interest in Brazil and to fragment the earlier consensus regarding race relations there.

The contrast between Ollie Stewart's accounts of his trip to Brazil in 1940 (Selection 13) and those of Robert S. Abbott in 1923 is stunning. The titles of some of Stewart's reports indicate his assessment of Brazilian race relations: "Afro Man Meets Brazil Prejudice"; "In U.S.A. It's Jim Crow; in Brazil, 'Run Around' "; "Brazil Rates Hair First." Stewart's essays, however, brought an angry rebuttal from a long-time Brazil enthusiast, James W. Ivy (Selection 14).[1] Ivy's defense of Brazil's social democracy was supported by Los Angeles physician Thomas Roy Peyton (Selection 18) and the prominent scholar Lorenzo D. Turner (Selection 20), both of whom had lived in Brazil for several months. George S. Schuyler's trip to South America in 1948, however, led him to write a very negative report on Brazil for the *Pittsburgh Courier* (Selection 19), similar in many ways to Stewart's assessment earlier in the decade.

The remaining items in Part II are by two of the nation's leading sociologists, W.E.B. Du Bois and E. Franklin Frazier. In a letter written in 1941 (Selection 15) Du Bois viewed Brazil very differently than he had in 1914

(Selection 4). Black Americans had long seen the gradual amalgamation of whites, Indians, and blacks in South America as a positive development. Du Bois had not challenged this attitude in 1914, but in 1941 he warned that absorption of the Negro through interracial mating was not only biologically difficult, but culturally and politically damaging for African people in South America and the world as a whole. Miscegenation had not enhanced the power of blacks or the value associated with Africanness in Brazil and it was not going to do so elsewhere, he advised.

E. Franklin Frazier's articles, one written for a non-scholarly audience and another for social scientists, show a leading student of race relations struggling with the question of Brazil.[2] When he observed elsewhere that it was "exceedingly difficult" to explain race relations in Brazil to North Americans,[3] he could well have been referring to the problem he himself encountered. His article "Brazil Has No Race Problem" (Selection 16), published in the liberal monthly *Common Sense*, was notably more complimentary regarding Brazil than the scholarly essay published virtually at the same time, "A Comparison of Negro–White Relations in Brazil and the United States" (Selection 17). But even in the *Common Sense* essay one finds contradictory assessments, reflecting the mid–twentieth century debate over the nature of Brazilian race relations in black America,[4] a debate in which black and white Americans and Brazilians took part.

NOTES

1. Stewart responded to Ivy in "Ollie Stewart Defends His Own Reports of What He Saw Down in Brazil," *Baltimore*

Afro-American, August 24, 1940. James H. Burney of Newport, Rhode Island, also disagreed with Stewart, "Says Ability Not Color Counts Most in Brazil," *Baltimore Afro-American*, August 31, 1940.

2. Frazier's assessment of Afro-Brazilian culture, like his view of race relations, was controversial. Frazier's assertion that in Brazil, as in the U.S., few African cultural influences survived was rejected by a leading white anthropologist, Melville J. Herskovits. See Herskovits's criticism of Frazier and Frazier's response in the *American Sociological Review* 8 (August 1943), 394–404.

3. E. Franklin Frazier, "Some Aspects of Race Relations in Brazil," *Phylon* 3 (1942), 291.

4. Another leading social scientist, Irene Diggs, who spent seven months in South and Central America, including one month in Brazil in the mid-1940s, also struggled in evaluating race relations in Brazil. See her article "How South America Thinks About Race," *Negro Digest* 5 (August 1947), 52–56. See also the two-part feature story on Brazil written in 1965 by Era Bell Thompson, "Does Amalgamation Work in Brazil?" *Ebony* 20 (July 1965), 27–41; and 20 (September 1965), 33–42. Brazil, she concluded, was neither a Negro haven nor a Negro hell. Yet despite disturbing evidence of racism, she answered the question posed in the title of her report positively: "Amalgamation may not be the complete answer to the racial problem, but so far it is the best. Should a serious problem of racial discrimination develop in Brazil they have the framework of a solution, the temperament to cope with matters racial and a law to prosecute those who violate the Brazilian concept of justice for all."

13.

Ollie Stewart, "The Color Line in South America's Largest Republic"

> *Ollie Stewart (b. 1906) was born in Louisiana and graduated from Tennessee State College in 1930. Before becoming a journalist he was by turns a stevedore, chauffeur, sailor, farm hand, and professional baseball player. He served as war correspondent for the* Baltimore Afro-American *during World War II. The series of articles on Brazil written for the* Afro-American *in 1940 was based on a twenty-day visit.*

"Afro Man Meets Brazil Prejudice" (June 22, 1940)

I HAVE NOW spent two whole days in Brazil. As I sit down to write this, a series of amazing, amusing, contradictory and almost unbelievable events have put so much pressure on the boy from Louisiana that whatever comes from this typewriter and makes sense is an accident. . . .

The food is good, my Spanish is sufficient to get me by, the weather is swell and the girls are gorgeous but that

From the *Baltimore Afro-American*, June 22 and 29, July 6 and 27, 1940. Reprinted by permission of the Afro-American Newspapers, Baltimore, Maryland.

ugly thing known as the color line has reared up to smack me squarely in the face.

Exactly eleven hotels have refused to give me a room since I set foot on Brazilian soil. The clerk at every one said the place was filled up. But I later called two by telephone—and found that I could get a place. I didn't try the others, but I have it on good authority that they ordinarily wouldn't be full during this, the off season.

Hotels Refuse Me

On the boat, a white Brazilian told me to try the Pax, the Natal, the Gloria and the Central. I tried them all and got a flat refusal. Then I tried the Astoria, the Flamengo and a half dozen others—with the same result. Maybe I am too black even for Brazilian tolerance.

Here's the story as it happened.

I had no trouble with the immigration authorities when they came aboard, and soon after the gangplank was down, I rushed ashore and had a porter to drag my stuff into the customs building. The examination of my bags took less than two minutes, and before one-third of the passengers were off the Argentina, I was in a cab and riding away.

Back to Water Front

And did I ride. I told the driver to take me to the Hotel Natal first. No luck there. To the Pax. Same thing. Then to six or seven other hotels in rapid succession, until the driver could think of no more. I was hot and tired and mad as hell, so I told him to take me back to the waterfront. There's always a hotel for sailors, I reasoned, and I figured that was my best bet.

I was right. The Europa Hotel took me in, and the price was seventy-five cents a night. It was a dump, but I was glad to be accepted. So I spent my first night in the Europa, frequented mostly by sailors—and people making a one-night stand in the love parade.

Next morning I set out to find another place. I walked about five miles. I walked damn near all over Rio de Janeiro. I went back to all the hotels that had refused me. I went to several new ones. And finally the Hotel Ouro Preto took me in. And now that I'm in it, I'm glad the others turned me down.

Cotton-Color Darkest

Ouro Preto is nice—even if nobody in it but me speaks English. It is Portuguese from top to bottom—and the darkest person in it is the color of cotton. All, that is, except me. My room on the third floor faces the bay, there's a park beneath my window, a café below, and the service is good.

The Europa did one thing for me, however. It introduced me to John. I don't know his last name. Just John—and the fact that he speaks English. It was he who asked me if I were an American the moment I walked into the Europa, and for the next two days did all my talking. He even followed me when I moved to the Ouro Preto.

John says he is a navigator, with four years of West Point behind him and a job that pays more than three hundred a month. Of course, the fact that I let him have a quarter (because he said he didn't have a cent) is no reflection on his truthfulness.

He's Super Pilot

You see, John was born in Rio, but moved to the States at an early age and is now an American citizen. His job, he says, is to take ships from one part of the world to the other. Something like a pilot, only he stays with the ship after it leaves the shore line and channel waters. There are, he tells me, only three colored men with jobs like his.

At any rate, his knowledge of Portuguese saved me the first two days—and his thirst for beer damn near broke me.

"There's no such thing as color in Brazil," John keeps telling me. "Everything is mixed up—black with white and white with black!"

Maybe he is right. That's what everybody tells me. But I keep remembering how many hotels got full in a hurry when I tried to get a room. I keep remembering that certain streets, certain parts of Rio and certain casinos have been all-white these two days I've been here, and certain others have been mostly peopled with dark persons.

"In U.S.A. It's Jim Crow; in Brazil, 'Run Around'" *(June 29, 1940)*

There's something wrong with the way the world views black people. There's something wrong with the way Brazil, the United States, the West Indies, Africa—everywhere—view black people. And the thing that's wrong in one place is the same thing that's wrong in every place.

Black people allow themselves to be kicked around by whites. Black people take any kind of treatment—and they take it sitting down. They're humble, they're too nice, have too many scruples and too damn much religion. I'm beginning to hate a mirror.

Brazil has opened my eyes. Segregation, discrimination and jim crow tactics—these things are not a matter of place. They can't be escaped by running from one place to another. They are hatched, they feed and flourish on the black man's capacity to keep taking it. And if anybody thinks the white man won't keep dishing it out as long as he can get away with it, that person needs to see some of the things I've seen here.

Traded Jim Crow

I was anxious to visit Brazil because of a report that Brazil had no color line or color prejudice. But I have made my last search for the fountain of youth. I traded the U.S. jim crow for the Brazilian run-around—and I shall be satisfied henceforth to do my bit toward getting my native house in order.

The American colored man can't solve his problem by running off to Cuba, Santo Domingo or Brazil. The white man in far-away places gives him the same going-over he took in New York, Maryland or Alabama. It's not the place; it's how long will you take it where you are?

I've been talking to a lot of people here in Rio these last few days and weeks. And just about the saddest tale I've heard came from a young Brazilian who wants to run away to a place where the colored man gets a square deal. If it hadn't been so tragic, I could have laughed.

Wants to Go to Tuskegee

He wants to go to Tuskegee. He wants to go to Tuskegee so badly that he's prepared to do anything—and he has already tried almost everything to get there. His home is in Santos, twelve hours by train from Rio. He has worked there to get money, he has starved himself sick in Rio, he has begged and written to at least fifty persons and foundations in the States for money—and hasn't a third of his boat fare.

Tuskegee would solve all his problems—he thinks. Booker T. Washington was the greatest man who ever lived —in his estimation. A Tuskegee education would make him equal to the white people who refused him admittance to the University of Brazil—so he says. Such faith! Such credulity! I almost wish he might have the chance to examine the pot of gold to be found at the end of an Alabama rainbow. It would do him good.

Here he is in Brazil, dying to get to Alabama to escape the awful hell of a color bar. A few years ago I was working at Tuskegee—and nothing would satisfy me but to get away to South America where I could be a free man.

The farce is very clear to me now. We are like dogs chasing our tails. We run from our shadows—but we never stop to think that if we sat down where we are, we wouldn't make such a tall shadow.

Both Want to Change

Yesterday I talked with a West Indian woman, from Barbados. "Ten years ago," she told me, "I left home to better my condition. I decided on Brazil and my sister went to New York. Now I'd give anything even to get back to Barbados—not to mention New York. But, you know one thing?—and it's a funny thing, too—my sister in New York wants to know how it is down here. She wants to make a change."

Brazil, she told me later in the conversation, is hell on earth for colored people. Colored are now being replaced with whites, and when you get out of a job, it's just too bad. There is no relief bureau, no WPA, no social security or unemployment insurance.

Clerks, chemists and ordinary white-collar jobs, she said, get only twenty dollars a month. Porters and maids get even less, if you can imagine such a thing. In some of the beautiful parks, they don't even want dark people to walk. If there are two brothers, one light and one dark, the light one will leave home in order not to have anything to do with the dark one.

Florida Heaven to Her

Today, I talked with a dark girl who was born in Miami. She came here three years ago as a nurse with a white family. She lost her job and would now sell her soul to get back to Florida. And any day Florida looks like heaven to anybody, they must be in an awful spot.

Incidentally, both this girl and the older woman hope to get boat fare by catching the lottery for a few hundred dollars. I hope they make it.

A young man who is connected with a progressive front movement told me that the worst thing that could happen to any individual is to be born black in Brazil. You can't get a decent job, you can't get a college or a university education, and you are destined to remain in the gutter.

Blames Two Things

He blames two things: the Catholic Church and the light-skinned colored man. The church teaches that it is wrong to make trouble or to question the acts of the Lord's anointed, which means the white man; and the mulatto, in his fight to get on the white bandwagon, kicks his dark brother around even more vigorously than the ofay.

"What the black Brazilian needs," he said, "is to follow the example of the American colored man. He should read American newspapers, magazines and books. He should have regular contact with the most advanced colored group the world has ever known. But, unfortunately, the American colored man does not give a damn about his Brazilian brother!"

"Brazil Rates Hair First" (July 6, 1940)

If it isn't a sin against the Holy Ghost, it is at least the height of bad judgment to be born black.

That is the conclusion I have come to after getting acquainted with Rio—one of the most beautiful places in the world, and the city I have tried harder to like than any place I've been.

Brazil has a hell of a color line. And it seems to be drawn according to the kind of hair you've got. The Portuguese and Indians come pretty dark sometimes, but they have straight hair. So they go anywhere and do anything. The mulatto, mixed African and Indian, or Portuguese and African, has long curly hair. So he gets by.

He Catches the Devil

But the plain colored man with short hair catches the devil!

Oh, they are very nice about giving colored people

the run-around. All smiles and we're-all-brothers-you-can-depend-on-that—but you find yourself on the outside looking in, just the same, if you ain't got that hair.

When the colored child gets to high school, he or she begins to get the works. Certain courses are suggested as "in their line," and others are practically forbidden them. Only the smartest, the ones with considerable money behind them and the guts to take it, get to the universities in and around Rio.

I spent half a day watching college students and university students pass in and out of classes. And I saw fewer colored than I would see on an average day at Harvard or New York University. Columbia or Chicago University have three times as many colored as the University of Brazil.

None Past High School

In other States the situation is worse. In São Paulo, the second city of Brazil, with a million population, where most of Brazil's wealth and industry is located, and where the coffee barons live, colored children are not allowed in schools past the high school level—and not too many get that far.

Most of the avenues for cultural achievements being closed to them, then, the colored Brazilian goes to work on lower levels. And because these levels pay only a subsistence wage, the dark brother rarely ever has money enough to see the opera, or to gamble at the casinos or to lie on the beach or to ride in fine cars or to dine at swank restaurants. He is told that he is welcome there—but the trick was turned when the money was kept out of his hands.

The same situation obtains in the deep South—except

that in the South they are frank enough to tell you to stay away if you're black.

The difference between New York and Rio is that nobody is colored in Rio unless he has short hair. The mulattoes are considered white. In New York, these same people would be colored, just as Mordecai Johnson of Howard is colored or Ralph Cooper or the Rev. A. Clayton Powell. All three would be white in Brazil.

If the same people who have the color and hair to make them white in Rio, and if all the people who look like them, could be white in New York, Sugar Hill would be a white neighborhood. The *Afro* would be practically a white newspaper.

One Drop vs. Few Drops

What I'm trying to say is this: One drop of colored blood makes you colored in the States; a few drops of white blood make you white in Brazil. So, although there are more colored people than white in Brazil, more than half of them are light enough to be classed as white. The third of the population that's left is like the bear—exactly nowhere!

One thing is true in Brazil, however, that has no counterpart in the States. Officers in the navy, the army, the police force and the fire department are more likely to be colored than white.

At every important building you see a soldier with a gun, standing guard. Usually he has a dark skin. Most of the officers directing traffic, most of the firemen with their spike-studded blue hats and most of the sailors are colored. There seems to be no discrimination when it comes to driving the buses, running the street cars or working on the docks. But most of the stores are run by white men.

Few "White" Menials

The men and women who carry heavy loads up and down the streets on top of their heads, are invariably black, and you very seldom see a white servant scrubbing and cleaning in front of the hotels. . . .

"Can Hitler Take Possession of Brazil?" *(July 27, 1940)*

After almost three weeks of poking my nose into various Brazilian corners, I shall try to summarize and draw a few very definite conclusions.

First of all, Brazil is absolutely controlled by a dictator. The work of President Getúlio Vargas [President of Brazil, 1930–45, 1951–54] is law, and make no mistake about it. Many persons will tell you that he is a kind man, interested in the welfare of his people and scornful of graft.

But there are almost as many who, if you can guarantee their safety, will whisper that the man is a tyrant.

Need United States Cash

In Brazil you hear much about the Good Neighbor Policy, but it is my opinion that the powers that be are jealous to the point of hatred where the United States is concerned. I also heard that the only reason Brazil keeps on good terms with the U.S. is that it becomes necessary to borrow money from Uncle Sam every now and then.

Brazil also has to import automobiles and many mechanical and electrical fixtures it has not learned to manufacture. Few as possible are bought from the States. Germany is the preferred market, and if the war hadn't come along, Uncle Sam was well on the way to being frozen out.

The fact remains, however, that a few big American concerns have huge sums of money invested in Brazil. They have so much money in banks, automobiles, motion pictures, radio equipment and factory parts that they can dictate policy. White Brazilians don't like it, but their hands are tied. They need money and machinery.

Most from the South

Colored Brazilians, as soon as they wake up, will not like it either, but for a different reason. Most American investors are from Miami and the South, and day by day they are teaching Brazil how to make a very definite place for the colored man at the bottom of the heap, and to keep him there.

In an earlier article I mentioned the fact that Brazil's color bar was a run-around. Brazil told its dark people that they were free to do what anybody else did, then promptly made it impossible for an ignorant, untrained and poverty-ridden man to get out of the gutter.

Some Few Try

Recently, however, a few unconquerable souls have tried to do the impossible. They have tried to enter the universities, go into business and achieve white collar jobs. They are tired of being bus drivers and soldiers on very meager pay. They wanted to gamble at the casinos and live in Botafogo and Ipenema, the swank residential sections.

But when they tried it, they found that the American white man had already set the standard; had already decided that the Lapa [an older, less-desirable area of Rio de Janeiro] was good enough for them.

So, instead of putting all of the blame for Brazil's color prejudice on Brazil—as I did in my first one or two articles—I am forced to credit some of the hellishness to American crackers. And knowing them as I do, I should have given them credit from the beginning.

There's Still Hope

Remembering all I have seen and heard in Rio, Santos, São Paulo and out in the country, I am not discouraged completely about the colored man's fate in Brazil. There are millions of them who do not yet have the white complex. But at the same time there are millions who have no vision.

Colored Americans should remedy this last condition!

They could make a start by visiting Brazil. I think part of the reason I was tossed out of so many hotels was the fact that it isn't customary for persons as dark as I am to walk into the big hotels loaded down with a big wad of milreis. It just isn't supposed to be done. Only rich white people do that. But—

If a few colored Americans had investments in Brazil, if twenty or thirty colored people from a ship barged into Copacabana with money to spend, I firmly believe that they would get accommodations. I am further convinced that if it were generally known in Brazil that there are colored people in the States who own banks, big farms, newspapers, insurance companies and are presidents of universities, colored travelers and colored Brazilians might get a better break.

Pioneering Profitable

Pioneering can be done profitably in Brazil. Matte—a new kind of tea—is almost a virgin enterprise. It was unknown in the States previous to 1933, but at the present time Americans consume about a third of the 90 thousand tons produced. Argentina buys a third, and Brazil drinks the rest.

I tried it hot, and later cold, and found it a delicious drink either way. The national Matte Institute in New York, at 505 Fifth Avenue, even gives away samples to help stimulate a demand for matte in the States. It is the principal cash crop of the Paraná region in Brazil, where most of the inhabitants are dark.

One enterprising young man asked me how he could best go about interesting colored American business men in exploiting matte, and I had to confess that, like myself, most Americans, black and white, had never heard of matte.

Must Visit Brazil

I told him, however, that it couldn't be done by remote control. His big job would be, I explained, to get an American colored man interested enough to even make a trip to Brazil. And I still think I told him the truth.

Other business opportunities in Brazil center around

the butterfly trade. Butterfly wings are used to decorate half of the bric-a-brac in Brazilian homes, and the trade with tourists is enormous.

Then there are the Bahia dolls, famous around the world. Carmen Miranda's famous costume in New York was simply the Sunday dress of the natives of Bahia, and most of the songs she sang were folk tunes from Bahia, which is inhabited almost entirely by blacks.

Bahia is in the northern part of Brazil, and I was told by several people that it is entirely different from southern Brazil, around Rio. There is no color problem because most of the people are colored, and practically control the region.

But I discovered at the Propaganda Department that the government does not encourage visitors to touch Bahia when they go into the interior. You have to have a pretty good reason before you will be issued a permit. Perhaps they don't want the natives to get ambitious. . . .

On the boat coming down was a young white fellow just out of the University of Oklahoma. His father-in-law brought him down to cut his eye teeth as a clerk in an importing firm. In a couple of years, he told me, he hoped to be manager. Then he could return to the States and make his experiences pay him a princely dividend.

Thinking about him made me wonder why colored professional and business men (even teachers) don't catch a boat now and then to scratch the surface in Brazil, Argentina, Central America or other West Indian islands. It is quite possible that some of them might discover potential investments.

Let Youngsters Try It

And if they don't feel like leaving home, why the hell can't they stake some young college graduate—their own son—maybe, to a chance to try his wings in Latin America?

America is rich because it sells and buys from other nations. America's reputation is made by the white men with money who buy and sell. This is particularly true of Brazil. But why must the word American be synonymous with white?

Why must all of the fortunes made in Latin America (in coffee, bananas, coconuts, rubber, tobacco and manufactured products) be made by white men.

Colored people have stores as outlets, trained young people to be clerks, salesmen and businessgetters. The colored group has men with money. All it needs is a handful of vision and a whole lot of guts!

Would Have to Take It

For pioneers always catch hell. A colored man trying to get a toehold in business in Brazil or Santo Domingo or Haiti today would have to take plenty. But American whites take it. Germans take it. Englishmen take it.

The only thing the average colored man will take is a picket sign—after the white man has sweated blood to build up a business that he has every right to build!

I reiterate, Brazil is almost a virgin land. It is young, undeveloped, full of hot blood and just about at the crossroads. In a few more years the pattern for the behavior of colored Brazilians will have been cut. Color bars are rapidly going up in many lines of endeavor, but immediate and aggressive action could topple a few and prevent others from being erected. . . .

"Brazil's Army Seems to Be All Colored"
(August 10, 1940)

If I have seemed bitter while writing about the color line, it is because what I found was such a shock to me. I expected to be able to go anywhere my money would take me. I expected to see unions between white men and Indians, Indians and colored women, colored men and white women. I expected to see colored men in business, colored boys flocking into the universities, and colored girls sipping drinks at the sidewalk tables.

And what did I see?

I saw universities for whites, fine hotels for whites, cafés and theatres for whites, business places run by whites, colored women for whites—but no white women for either colored men or Indians. I saw the same reason for mulattoes that I have been seeing all my life in the South!

I saw colored men in the army and navy—many of them. I saw a colored general and many navy officers. I saw colored firemen and policemen and bus drivers and street car motormen and conductors. And for this tolerance I want to give full credit to Brazil—but I keep feeling there is a catch to it.

All these departments are rigidly controlled by the government. That man Vargas has them directly under his thumb. And the pay is very small—about twenty-five dollars a month.

If everything is on an equal basis, why were there no colored in the department of propaganda, agriculture, fine arts, commerce, amusement and business? The answer I got was that colored are not trained sufficiently for the big money jobs. I think it's the run-around.

Maybe I am over-suspicious, but I think the army and navy is [*sic*] practically all-colored because these branches provide cannon fodder when a revolution breaks out. Soldiers get killed while the man who gives orders lives to rake in the gravy. And the same thing applies to policemen. In Brazil they are national officers, becoming soldiers the moment trouble breaks out.

It's Not Tolerance

Yes, they wear uniforms. But they are barely able to eat. They cannot buy cars or buy homes near the beaches, or coffee plantations, or planes or business houses, on their salaries. I am convinced it isn't tolerance as much as it is a nice way to keep somebody on hand to pull the government's chestnuts out of the fire.

And my verdict is: I'd rather be colored in the United States. At least I know what I'm up against. Also, my children can go to college. And all the light-skinned women are not dying to marry a white man or have a child by him. In the latter respect, Brazil is just like Jamaica and Haiti.

The trip convinced me that the American colored man is ahead of any other colored group I have seen. Brazilians have the greatest opportunity, because they are so far behind.

14.

James W. Ivy, "Stewart in Error; No Color Line in Brazil"

> *James W. Ivy (1901–74) was a Virginia-born and -educated journalist and educator. After serving as book review editor for* The Crisis *from 1930 to 1942 and briefly as managing editor of* Common Sense *in the mid-1940s, he became assistant editor of* The Crisis *in 1946 and editor from 1950 to his retirement in 1966. Under his editorship the magazine published a number of articles on the position of blacks in Africa, Latin America, and elsewhere.*

SOME TRAVELERS, especially exploratory journalists with a racial chip on their shoulders, wander over the earth's surface for no other apparent reason than to be able to tell us afterwards how the desk clerk at the London Claridge or the Paris Ritz refused them accommodations, how they were not allowed to order a dry martini at "The King of Bohemia" in High Street, or how the doorman gently elbowed them out of the Au Poisson d'Or.

Yet in possibly the same paragraph they will tell how

From the *Baltimore Afro-American*, August 17, 1940. Reprinted by permission of the Afro-American Newspapers, Baltimore, Maryland.

well they were received in some exclusive bordel, say the Chez Famille. They may even study Brazilian color prejudice within the exclusive confines of the Urca Casino. Their travels are really a record of their discomforts and disappointments as aliens in a foreign land, not of discriminations which arise solely because of their race.

Short on History

Such peripatetic sociologists usually know nothing of the history, the language, the customs, or the habits of the country they so generously "write up." And because they are Americans whose vision has been warped by color they are prone to explain their personal difficulties as well as those of the natives solely in terms of race.

The *Afro*'s special correspondent in Brazil, Mr. Ollie Stewart, the wide-eyed country boy from Louisiana, is a striking illustration of this type of American traveler. In his very first paragraph of "In the U.S.A. It's Jim Crow; in Brazil, 'Run Around'" he pulls this gaffe:

"And the thing that's wrong in one place is the same thing that's wrong in every place."

This doesn't even make sense. And if he means that our problems are the same the world over, he's worse than naive; he's merely stupid.

Even in the U.S.A. our problem, despite the national ideology anent us, is not the same in New York City as it is in Atlanta, Ga.

"I was anxious to visit Brazil because of a report that Brazil had no color line or color prejudice." Brazil does not have a color line (in the American sense), Mr. Stewart to the contrary notwithstanding. And when Brazilian writers wish to describe the idea of a color line they usually use our American phrase.

Can't Prove Bar

Nor can Mr. Stewart prove the existence of a Brazilian color line by stressing the personal misfortunes of disgruntled expatriates. That there is some color prejudice in Brazil is a thing that has never been denied even by the Brazilians themselves, but it has never been erected into the color-caste system of the States.

What Mr. Stewart does not seem to know is that throughout Latin America class takes precedence over color. That few pure blacks, though there are many mulattoes, are found in this ruling caste is due solely to the fortuitous circumstances that slavery has placed us at the bottom of the social and economic scale. Brazilian history explains the African's position in Brazilian society without reference to his color.

Furthermore, if there is a "color line" in Brazil, Mr. Stewart is singularly unequipped to find it. On his own admission he knows no Portuguese. With this initial language handicap how can he find out anything worthwhile about Brazil and Brazilians? And with no knowledge of Brazilian history and customs how can he be expected to interpret even the obvious?

What's His Authority?

Moreover, who ever heard of a competent journalist interpreting the life of a country through the inconsequential chit-chat of bar-flies and down-at-the-heel inebriates?

What do we learn about the status of Brazilian colored people from a boy from Santos who is just dying to go to Tuskegee? And because James Bell, after ten years in Brazil, is homesick for the ghettoes of our American cities, it does not prove that the situation of the *preto* (Negro) in Os Estados Unidos do Brasil is on a par with that of those in the United States of North America.

And why this monotonous stressing of the unessential, the universal trivia of living? We are not interested in "Mama Yo Quero" (which incidentally is neither Portuguese nor Spanish), nor the Catholic dogma that we must [not] question "the acts of the Lord's anointed," nor that the mulatto fights to get on the white bandwagon (he does the same thing here), nor that night life in Rio is dull, nor that *rameira* [prostitutes] may be had for twenty-five cents (two bits).

What Stewart Resents

At bottom, what our naive Mr. Stewart seems to resent is the idea that there are places in the world where the colored man does not occupy the same pariah status which he has in the States. His is the point of view which will make a terrorized colored person in Atlanta, Ga., argue that New York City treats the Aframerican no better than the uniformed Kluxers of the Atlanta police force.

Or that a colored "university" in the Deep South is the equal of Harvard or Yale. Now what is the real status of the ex-African slave in Brazil? Are Brazilian *brancos* (whites) the same race haters of our Deep South?

The answer, of course, is no. Brazil has no "color line" in the American sense. And Brazil has freely accepted educated, cultured colored persons as members of Brazilian society, as human beings, as equals. So liberal are the Brazilians on the question of color that the Argentines call Brazil "a colored tropical republic."

What Is a "Negro"?

First, let us examine the Brazilian definition of "Negro," both for the benefit of your readers and the "*Afro*'s own correspondent." Contrary to American practice, the word "Negro" is accepted in its etymological and biological sense of a black man and not in the sociological sense in which it is accepted in the States. In Brazil a "Negro" is a *preto*, a black man; one obviously black in color.

The various mixed bloods are given other names, and if they are white in color they are accepted as white. No Brazilian would think of classifying Walter White[1] as a *preto* merely because he had some African great-great-grandparents.

Nor is it silly for a light-brown Brazilian of obvious African features to think of himself as other than white, since most of the white Brazilians have been liberally tar-brushed and Indian-bronzed. This is the explanation behind the Brazilian practice of ignoring the African blood of many famous Brazilians. Nilo Peçanha, a former president [from June 1909 to November 1910], and Machado de Assis, the famous *literateur*, are, for example, almost never mentioned as colored.

Examples of No Color Line

Only in a country without a color line could a colored man become that country's president. Only in a country without a color line could an African born during the slave period become that country's pioneer in Germanic studies and one of its great poets, as did Tobias Barreto.

Only a country without a color line would find its favorite poet in a Gonçalves Dias, an African.

Could a colored man be the father of psychiatry and the director general of the hospital for the insane in Rio if that country had a color line? Yet Juliano Moreira did just these things.

André Rebouças was a great engineer in Brazil while if he had lived in the States he would have been merely "another colored engineer."

Could It Happen Here?

Could America with its color line have a brilliant colored philosopher of the stamp of Farias Britto?

Would the color line of the States permit the existence of a brilliant thinker such as the black man Tito Livio de Castro?

Where is our General Tiburcio?

Where is our José do Patrocinio, our Father José Mauricio?

Isn't it strange that Brazil with her "color line" should have listed in the biographical section of Seguier's dictionary nineteen famous colored persons in contrast to the miserly three listed in the biographical section of Webster's? A whole book could be written on the colored persons famous in Brazil, men noted for their achievements as Brazilians and not, as in America, for their achievements as "colored persons."

How Does He Explain?

If there is a "color line" in Brazil how does Mr. Stewart explain the presence of black captains on Brazilian ships? A Brazilian ship in drydock in Newport News three weeks ago had a black captain.

When the Brazilian navy visited Old Point some years ago local whites were shocked at the idea of having to dance with the dusky officers. And yet Brazil has a *color line!*

How would Mr. Stewart explain Harry Franck's[2] remark that 70 percent of the Brazilians would have to ride jim crow in the South? Or the frequent irritation of ofay American travelers that the colored people are not put in their proper place in Brazil? Or *Life*'s frequent snide remarks that black Brazilians are accepted as the equals of their white brethren?

If a man makes it his duty to go around ferreting out racial prejudice, he will naturally find it.

Prejudices of all kinds exist everywhere, but not every country erects the collective phobias of one group of its citizens into a social and economic institution. Not every country makes a political creed of racial hate. And because some blacks have hard sledding in a country it does not follow that all blacks suffer. There are even classes among the colored people of Mr. Stewart's own Louisiana.

May Be Increasing

Perhaps color prejudice against the blacks is increasing in Rio, but the wide-eyed boy from the Louisiana bayous is the last person to discover it, or its real significance if it actually exists. Our innocent discovers the "run around" in one block and brags, like a typical southern peasant, how well he is treated in some swanky café or bar in the next block.

A boy from a southern ghetto doesn't know what to do with racial freedom. Because he longs for the racial bars of the States and doesn't find them in France or Brazil, he begins to fancy that they exist. He doesn't feel at home when he's not treated like an ex-slave.

If the wide-eyed Mr. Stewart will learn some Portuguese, bone up on Brazilian history and sociology, cut out his razzle-dazzle friends and homesick expatriates, get over his astonishment at licensed *mancebas* [prostitutes], and wonderment over the dogmas of the Catholic Church, he will then be in a position to tell us something valuable about the status of colored people in Brazil.

NOTES

1. A NAACP official from 1918 to 1955 who was blue-eyed and blond-haired, with such fair skin that he could "pass" for white.

2. A U.S. educator and author of travel books. Franck's statement was in *Working North from Patagonia* (New York, 1922), 200.

15.

Letter by W.E.B. Du Bois to Edward Weeks, Atlanta, Georgia, October 2, 1941

> *Edward Weeks was editor of the* Atlantic Monthly *from 1938 to 1966. In this letter Du Bois proposed two articles for publication in the* Atlantic Monthly, *"The Future of Europe in Africa" and "The Future of Africa in America." Neither was published in the magazine.*

... THERE IS needed a complete re-statement of the so-called American Negro problems with a frank facing of the methods in which they must be faced and the decisions that must be made. We know that there are some fourteen million persons in the United States of acknowledged Negro descent. We are quite aware that the population of the West Indies is overwhelmingly Negroid. In Latin-America there are 130 million inhabitants of whom 20 million, at least, are of Negro descent. Now what is to be the future of these peoples and their relations to each other?

In the United States we have gone far enough to know

Reprinted from *The Correspondence of W.E.B. Du Bois, Volume II, Selections, 1934–1944,* ed. by Herbert Aptheker (Amherst: University of Massachusetts Press, 1976), 304–5, copyright © 1976 by The University of Massachusetts Press.

that the ability which can be developed among persons of Negro descent, is of the widest range; that in physical, intellectual and artistic lines, the Negro is not only in evidence but if it were not for deliberate hindrances set-up to his development he would make even better showing. We know that his health and crime can be adequately explained by his poverty, and that increased income and education can without reasonable doubt raise the mass of the Negro people to or above the average level of their white neighbors.

But these very facts disclose a problem which the nation and the white is unwilling to face. Even with present barriers, if the Negro continues to develop at the present rate in the United States and Latin America, there is not a single door of human progress and of social recognition at which he is not going to knock with increasingly bitter violence. On the other hand, if the barriers are done away with, the Negro race in America is going to reach within a calculable time a high level of efficiency which will challenge the whole assumption of the natural superiority of the white race. It will take more and more deliberate effort on the part of whites to enforce caste restrictions. What now is going to be our policy?

In order to preserve our intellectual honesty and ethical pretensions this question must come in for frank discussion and decision. We cannot permit the Southern United States to be a social back-water in order to hold the Negro in his place. Neither can we allow the West Indies and Central America to be made deliberate slums for the profit and vacation activities of the whites. In South America we have long pretended to see a possible solution in the gradual amalgamation of whites, Indians and blacks. But this amalgamation does not envisage any decrease of power and prestige among whites as compared with Indians, Negroes and mixed bloods; but rather an inclusion within the so-called white group of a considerable infiltration of dark blood, while at the same time maintaining the social bar, economic exploitation and political disfranchisement of dark blood as such. We have thus the spectacle of Santo Domingo, Cuba, Puerto Rico and even Jamaica trying desperately and doggedly to be "white" in spite of the fact that the majority of the white group is of Negro or Indian descent. And despite facts, no Brazilian nor Venezuelan dare boast of his black fathers. Thus racial amalgamation in Latin-America does not always or even usually carry with it social uplift and planned effort to raise the mulatto and mestizoes to freedom in a democratic polity.

This problem of the African in America cannot be avoided. He is not dying out; and he is not likely to die out. His sudden physical absorption without planned social effort would result in a distinct lowering of the level of culture over wide areas. On the other hand, the attempt to raise the culture among the whites and lower or even retard it among the Negroes and mulattoes, is a task inexcusable if not impossible.

There is needed, therefore, in the Western world widespread consultation and planning, backed by united effort first to decide just how far we are willing to treat Negroes and mulattoes as human beings, and if not what open and tenable justification we have for denying it. If we are going to break down the barriers and at great cost in wealth and effort gradually raise this depressed class to the level of the culture of which they are capable, we must frankly understand that this does not mean the domination of a white world in the future; in fact, it is the beginning of the end of such domination. There is no moral question facing the Americas of greater and more pressing importance than this question of racial tolerance in the Western Hemisphere. . . .

16.
E. Franklin Frazier, "Brazil Has No Race Problem"

Edward Franklin Frazier (1894–1962) was born in Baltimore, Maryland, where he lived until enrolling in Howard University in 1912. After teaching secondary school in Baltimore, he earned a masters degree from Clark University in 1921, studied for a year in Denmark, and taught sociology at Morehouse College in Atlanta from 1922 to 1927. He received a Ph.D. in sociology from the University of Chicago in 1931. He did research and taught at Fisk University from 1929 to 1934 and then became head of the Department of Sociology at Howard University where he taught until his retirement in 1959. He was a leading scholar on the African American in the United States and a specialist on the Negro family. In 1948 he became the first black American to serve as president of the American Sociological Association.

The research upon which the following articles are based was conducted in Brazil over a five-and-a-half-month period in 1940–41. Frazier also wrote two other essays on Brazil: "Some Aspects of Race Relations in Brazil," Phylon 3 (1942), 287–95; and "Rejoinder" to Melville J. Herskovits, "The Negro in Bahia, Brazil: A Problem in Method," American Sociological Review 8

From *Common Sense* 11 (November 1942), 363–65.

(August 1943), 402–4. Frazier's assessment of the position of the Afro-Brazilian is discussed in David J. Hellwig, "E. Franklin Frazier's Brazil," Western Journal of Black Studies 15 (Summer 1991), 87–94.

THE PRESENT WAR has caused many thoughtful Americans to weigh the traditional policy of the United States in regard to the colored tenth of its population. This has been due partly to the general unrest among Negroes and their low morale. It has also resulted from the fact that our chief allies today are among the colored peoples of Asia and Africa. These people are watching us with suspicion because of our treatment of the American Negro and our attitude toward colored peoples in general. Even our relations with Latin-America, not to mention our relations with the Negroes in the West Indies, have been affected by our treatment of the American Negro. Brazil, with a large population of Negroes and persons of Negro descent, has been watching with interest the treatment of the Negro during recent years. On the other hand, we are beginning to give more serious attention to Brazil where despite its absolutely and relatively larger Negro or colored population there is no race problem in the American sense. The fortunate appearance at this time of Professor Donald Pierson's book, *Negroes in Brazil*,[1] which should be read by every intelligent American, is an indication of this interest. Therefore, it may be well to compare the racial situation in Brazil with that in the United States and see what may be learned from the "good neighbor" to the south of us.

Of course, in making a comparison between the racial situation in Brazil and in the United States, one must take account of the differences in the histories of the two countries, the differences in their economic development and in their political organization. But let us not make excuses of them.

Nearly thirty years ago Theodore Roosevelt observed that "the one point in which there is a complete difference between the Brazilian and ourselves" was the attitude toward the black man. Namely, in Brazil there is no stigma attached to Negro blood. "One drop of Negro blood" does not make a person a Negro and condemn him to become a member of a lower caste. A Negro or a person of Negro ancestry is able to acquire a place in the economic and social organization to which his skills and culture entitle him. Moreover, it is generally accepted as an unexpressed national policy that the Negro is to be absorbed into the total population. It was with this in mind that a Brazilian statesman reminded Roosevelt that in a hundred years Brazil would have no Negroes whereas the United States would have the problem of twenty or thirty million Negroes.

In the absence of race prejudice and color caste, the Negro and mixed-blood have come to occupy a place in Brazilian society that accords with their economic and social development or the degree and processes of assimilation of Brazilian culture. In the upper class, which is predominantly white, there are many mixed-bloods but relatively few blacks. The mixed-bloods predominate in the middle class and the blacks are more numerous than in the upper class. The vast majority of the blacks are to be found in the lower class along with mixed-bloods and a relatively few whites. This is the situation in northern Brazil where most of the Negroes settled and the same process operates throughout the country. The relation between class and color is what one would expect in a society based upon free competition instead of caste. The situation in northern Brazil corresponds very closely to that within the colored community in the United States. The mixed-bloods have enjoyed, in addition to a longer history of freedom, certain economic and cultural advantages similar to those enjoyed by the mulattoes in the United States. It should be pointed out, however, that the Negroes and mixed-bloods of Brazil have not enjoyed the benefits of philanthropy but have been forced to compete on an equal basis with whites.

The results of such a system of race relations are reflected in the character and personality of Negroes and persons of Negro descent in Brazil. The Brazilian Negro, to use the term in the American sense, first of all is a Brazilian. He is loyal to Brazil and harbors no resentments against whites. He has faith in the justice of the courts and he is convinced that his abilities and achievements will be recognized. He knows too that there is a single standard for all and that there are no easy or cheap short-cuts to fame and fortune in a segregated world. There is some color prejudice against those of black complexion but such prejudice is a personal matter and is not legalized or institutionalized. But no matter how poor or how humble his station in life, the Brazilian black does not cringe but is dignified and has a sense of personal worth. The whites on their part do not fear the competition of the Negro nor do they feel insecure in their social position. They do not make a fetish of racial purity and the superiority of white blood. They do not feel the need to organize mobs under the pretense of defending white womanhood nor do they make a travesty of justice under the pretense that it is necessary in order to maintain civilization and white supremacy. They realize that the ignorant and brutalized and segregated Negro would be a greater threat to civilization than the civilized Negro who is integrated into Brazilian society.

Our Jim-Crow Policy

Let us now turn to the United States where an attempt has been made to regulate the relations between the two races by establishing a rigid caste system based upon blood. Some writers have attempted to attribute the hostility between the two races in this country to the Civil War and Reconstruction. But even before the Civil War the free mulattoes and Negroes, many of whom had risen economically and culturally, were regarded with hostility and condemned to a subordinate caste. Since the Civil War our policy has been to shunt all persons of Negro descent to a segregated world and so long as they have not been considered a menace to the white world, whites have been indifferent to what they did. In a time of national crisis, such as the present war, when it is of concern to the larger white community what happens in the Negro world, then all the evils of segregation and caste become apparent. Today the country is faced with thirteen million colored citizens, the majority of whom are indifferent, restless, sullen, resentful and cynical because of the injustices which they have suffered.

The segregated Negro world in America is a pathological phenomenon which has pronounced in an acute form all the pathological phenomena that characterize social life.[2] Besides producing all the physical pathologies, segregation has distorted the Negro's outlook on life and has caused him to nurture resentments and to cultivate evasion and dissimulation as an art in order to survive. Not only do discussions of the Negro problem constantly fill the every-day conversations of Negroes but many Negro intellectuals bound by caste restrictions are articulate only when they are discussing the problem. The Negro's attitude toward politics, economic questions, class relations, religion, and war are all colored by his position in American life. Segregation and caste have created a double standard of achievement and efficiency which has affected adversely the Negro. In the Negro world the Negro has not been subjected to the competition that he would have been forced to meet in a society in which he was free. When friendly whites praise his achievements they generally entertain the unspoken reservation that it is good for a Negro. Whereas in Brazil a black man is an artist, writer, or scientist, in the United States he is always a "Negro artist" or "Negro scientist." Many Negroes are made great and important simply because they have the financial and moral support of whites and help to maintain the caste system. Consequently, ignorant and incompetent Negroes are placed in positions of authority and power in the Negro world. Only in the northern cities where the Negro is able to break through caste restrictions is he beginning to acquire the intellectual and moral stature and outlook of other Americans.

Unconscious Hypocrisy

In fact, the Negro has never been taken seriously or treated as a mature, intelligent human being. Practically every white person no matter how young or inexperienced or ignorant presumes to give advice to Negroes. For over a century whites have been trying to make Negroes believe that there is something essentially wrong with Negro blood. Even friendly whites counsel the Negro to develop race pride, conveniently forgetting the fact that at least two-thirds of the Negroes in the United States are of mixed ancestry. Despite the friendliness of the present Administration toward Negroes, it does not accept the judgments of mature, intelligent Negroes but, according to reports, has selected a liberal southern white as the final authority in matters pertaining to Negroes. The numerous Negro advisers connected with the various departments of government have no administrative power.[3]

Whatever justification there has been for treating the Negro as an immature person, incapable of sound judgments, has been due to the traditional system of race relations in the United States. The great masses of Negroes have been kept in a state of economic dependence and social subordination often maintained by terrorizing the Negro. The natural leaders among Negroes who have dared to show any independence in thought or action have been driven out of the South. Since most Negro leaders have been forced to make their living behind the walls of segregation, the threat of starvation has been sufficient to bring submission. It might be said that the Negro has been subjected to a process of dysgenic selection. Many of those who have found a place in the institutional set-up within the Negro world have become emasculated or cynical. Character develops only where men are accustomed to responsibilities and Negroes have never been required or permitted to assume serious responsibilities. The most serious responsibility imposed upon many Negro leaders has been to beg alms from whites for educational and welfare institutions. Negro men of character, that is men possessing courage and convictions and a willingness to live and die for what they believe are found as often in the underworld of our cities as in the ranks of respectable

Negro leaders. In other words the whole system of race relations in America has tended to rob the mass of Negroes of a sense of personal worth and dignity and to rob their leaders of character.

The "Uplift" Movement

As if to compensate for the denial of freedom and justice, America has through its philanthropies spent millions of dollars in uplifting the Negro. But this has failed to solve the fundamental problem of integrating the Negro into the American economic and social life. Some writers feel that oppression and prejudice have given the Negro an incentive to rise and improve himself. But if we apply the definition of a Negro used in the United States to Brazil, we find that under a system of free competition the Negro in Brazil has out-stripped the Negro in the United States. Despite all the philanthropy and inter-racial work, Negroes and white people still do not know each other after three hundred years of association. Whereas in Brazil white, brown and black people know each other as individual human beings, white people in the United States only know the Negro as a symbol or stereotype. Only in the North where Negroes and whites do occasionally form friendships on the basis of mutual attraction and mutual interests are truly human relations between the races established.

All of this points to one conclusion: caste and democracy cannot exist in the same society without perpetual conflict. This is indicated in every genuine attempt to ameliorate the racial situation and to bring about peace in race relations; namely, an attempt is made to remove caste restrictions which prevent the Negro from competing as a free member of society. It appears that we have chosen the painful way, involving a tremendous economic and social waste, of integrating the Negro into the economic and social organization. Some of the Negro's so-called white friends and "safe" leaders are advising him not to use the war emergency to improve his status. The Negro is wise enough not to be mis-led by such "sober counsel" for he knows from bitter experience that only in a crisis situation has his status been improved. Whether he wishes it or not, he has been forced to improve his status through the conflict process. For example, any sane person knew that there was no justification for paying Negro teachers less than white teachers; but it was necessary to fight the issue out in the courts. Thus the Negro must continue to fight for his right because we have accepted the principle of caste in race relations instead of the principle of free competition. Our attitude toward the question of race is due partly to our provincial outlook. Our provincialism in regard to race relations may be broken down as we are forced to treat with the colored peoples of Asia and become more closely tied to Latin-America. On the other hand, it is conceivable that we may attempt to impose our attitudes upon these peoples. If the latter happens then we shall not be able to assume moral leadership in the post-war world and will alienate the countries of Latin-America. While we may provide Brazil with technical skill and capital, Brazil has something to teach us in regard to race relations.

NOTES

1. Donald Pierson, *Negroes in Brazil: A Study of Race Contact at Bahia* (Chicago, 1942). Frazier had a high regard for Pierson's work, which supported the myth of the racial

paradise. See the reviews of the book written by Frazier in *The American Journal of Sociology* 48 (November 1942), 434–35; *The Negro Quarterly* 1 (Winter/Spring 1943), 380–81; and *Annals of the American Academy of Political and Social Science* 227 (May 1943), 188–89. Pierson assisted Frazier during his visit to Brazil in many ways.

2. Frazier's assessment of African-American society and especially the black family as pathological has been challenged by many. For an able summary of the controversy, see G. Franklin Edwards, "E. Franklin Frazier," in *Black Sociologists: Historical and Contemporary Perspectives*, ed. James E. Blackwell and Morris Janowitz (Urbana, Ill., 1975), 94–101.

3. The leading southern white liberal on racial issues in the Roosevelt administration was Will Alexander, head of the Farm Security Administration and during World War II director of the Minority Groups Service in the Office of Production Management. For a discussion of the views and activities of Alexander and other southern white liberals during the New Deal, see John B. Kirby, *Black Americans in the Roosevelt Era: Liberalism and Race* (Knoxville, Tenn., 1980), 48–75.

17.

E. Franklin Frazier, "A Comparison of Negro–White Relations in Brazil and the United States"

THERE IS, in Brazil, little discussion of the racial or the color situation. It appears that there is an unexpressed understanding among all elements in the population not to discuss the racial situation, at least as a contemporary phenomenon. Apparently, there is a general recognition that Brazil is essentially a country of mixed-bloods and that a new ethnic type is being formed. Oliveira Vianna [1] is a rare exception among the scholars, in that he regards both Indians and Negroes as inferior races and believes that, through Aryanization or a whitening process, Brazil will become a white nation. Although there is no race problem in Brazil, the upper classes are conscious of color differences and these color differences become the basis of social distances that are maintained by a subtle system of etiquette. In fact, these distinctions would escape the casual observer and, even when one discovers them, it is dangerous to generalize about them. If one should suggest an American situation analogous to the situation in Bahia, one might point to the colored community in Charleston

From *Transactions of the New York Academy of Sciences*, 2d ser., vols. 6–7 (May 1944), 265–69. Reprinted by permission of the Annals of the New York Academy of Sciences, New York, New York.

and New Orleans, forty or fifty years ago. Bahia is essentially a mulatto community where persons of light complexion tend to dissociate themselves as much as possible from those of dark or black complexion. Of course, this does not preclude friendships between whites and blacks. According to a lawyer of pure Portuguese ancestry, members of his group are likely to be more free and friendly with blacks than the mixed-bloods. It is not unusual for whites or so-called whites to marry people of light-brown and brown complexion. In such cases, the brown-skin people are likely to become essentially white persons, or at least the children of such unions would be regarded as white. In fact, one of the reasons that it is impossible to draw a color line, not only in the north but in other parts of Brazil, is because it would cut across families.

The prejudice toward black persons seems to operate most strongly in intimate social relations involving marriage and in the new type of social life which is developing in clubs and hotels. For example, black persons do not attend the weekly dances at the large hotels patronized by Brazilian officials and business men as well as foreigners; nor are black men to be found at the tennis clubs and the yacht clubs. They may attend on some special occasion, but they do not move about freely and they would not be invited to become members. Of course, if they marry a white person, their children would be eligible for membership provided their parents belonged to the upper economic classes. Since foreign whites frequent the hotels and the clubs, it may be asked, to what extent are they responsible for these attitudes toward the blacks? Undoubtedly, the British and the Americans would not care to have black people in these places and some Brazilians are sensitive to their attitudes in regard to blacks. But the foreigners are not entirely nor primarily responsible for the attitudes toward blacks. They reflect the attitudes of the mixed-bloods who seek to identify themselves with the whites. What has been said so far applies to the upper social and economic strata in Bahia. Color distinctions and prejudices against the blacks are seemingly absent on the whole from the mind of the masses. This is apparent not only in their everyday activities but in the numerous festivals where all colors mingle freely. In fact, it is among the laboring masses that race mixture is continuing on a large scale in Brazil.

In the states São Paulo, Santa Catarina, and Paraná in southern Brazil, color prejudice is much more marked than in the north. These are the states to which have come large numbers of European immigrants—chiefly German and Italian—who have a different attitude toward the Negro from that of the Portuguese. In these areas, the Negro, especially the dark or black person of Negro descent, has become a conspicuous minority in a predominantly white population. In this region, the attitude toward the Negro assumes often the character of race prejudice as opposed to color prejudice. Although there are no legal discriminations against persons of Negro blood, they are isolated and discriminated against in subtle ways. From conversations with some of the leaders among the blacks, it appeared that the Negro suffers chiefly from the economic competition of the European immigrant, especially the Italian. As the Negro is pushed down in the economic scale, he is unable to acquire the education and the skills which would enable him to compete successfully with other groups. The only escape for the Negro is to mingle his blood with that of the whites. This he is doing, though not as freely as in other parts of Brazil.

Because of the isolation of the Negro in the south,

a number of Negro organizations have come into existence to fight discrimination on the basis of color. Out of these various organizations has come Frente Negra Brasileira, which was started in 1931 as a movement to include all Negroes in Brazil. In this year, the organization announced, at a meeting of over a thousand Negroes, its program for the improvement of the moral, educational, economical, and political status of the Negro. It was recognized by the government as a political party but, after the changes in the government in 1937, it retained only the cultural and social features of its program. Besides the Frente Negra Brasileira, a number of other Negro clubs and associations have been organized in the south and in other parts of Brazil.[2] The organizations in the south are sharply differentiated from those in the north. In the south, they are fighting discrimination and are seeking to integrate themselves into the social and economic organization. On the other hand, in the north, they have cooperated with whites in studying the cultural contributions of the Negro and have fought for religious liberty for Negro cults, as well as the improvement of the social condition of blacks. It appears that the Negro organizations in Brazil lack the drive and motivation of similar organizations in the United States. This is doubtless due to the fact that racial discrimination is not as strong even in southern Brazil as in the United States. In São Paulo, where a number of these movements originated, there are two Negro professors on the law faculty of the University. It appears that amalgamation will constantly undermine these Negro movements unless outside influences affect present tendencies.

Outside influences certainly have had some effect upon attitudes toward colored and black people. Many Brazilians are conscious of being regarded as a colored nation by Argentina and other so-called white nations of South America. Then, in recent years, Nazi racial theories have had some influence among the Germans in the south who tended to intermarry with the Brazilians. The most important source of outside influence has been the financial and industrial penetration of the country. The British and the Americans draw a color line, not only in their social contacts with Brazilians, but when their business houses employ Brazilians as white collar workers. Americans who have gone to Brazil as technical advisers have insisted that even distinguished black officials be ejected from hotels and, when their wishes were not respected, they have left the hotels. In spite of the "good neighbor" policy, it is likely that increasing financial and industrial penetration of Brazil by Americans will accentuate discrimination on the basis of color. Even at the present time, Brazilians are careful to select pictures of the right complexion for the American public.

In spite of these differences between the racial situation in Brazil and the United States, it should be pointed out by way of conclusion that the development of race relations in the two countries reveals some underlying similarities. In both countries, the close association of the whites and blacks produced a class of mixed-bloods. Although, in the United States, an attempt to maintain a caste system has prevented the identification of the mixed-bloods with the whites; through the process of "passing," persons with Negro blood have passed into the white race. With the increasing mobility of our population, it is likely that this will continue. It is hardly probable that the so-called "race purity" laws of Virginia and Georgia will stop the process. Race mixture in the United States, as in Brazil, has been one of the chief factors in the social differentiation of the non-white population, and it has facilitated the social mobility of colored individuals. The relation of color differences to occupational structure in Brazil closely parallels the same phenomenon in the segregated Negro community in the United States. Moreover, as in Brazil, this phenomenon in the United States is a rough index to the process of acculturation, though it does not lead to complete assimilation, because of the attempt to maintain a racial caste in the United States. As the attempt to maintain a caste system becomes less effectual because of urbanization and the general educational and cultural development of the Negro, it is likely that the racial situation will approximate the situation in Brazil.

NOTES

1. Vianna, a self-taught sociologist, wrote *Evolução do Povo Brasileiro* (Evolution of the Brazilian people) in 1933 and *Raça e Assimilacão* (Race and assimilation) in 1934. Frazier published a review of the first book in the *American Journal of Sociology* 41 (March 1936), 674–75.

2. Frazier brought back to the United States a message from the National Union of Men of Color of São Paulo addressed to their "brothers" in North America that sharply attacked the treatment of Negroes in Brazil. A translation was published as "A Message to American Negroes" in *Phylon* 3 (1942), 284–86, along with Frazier's essay "Some Aspects of Race Relations in Brazil"; Frazier made no reference to it in his published essays on Brazil.

18.

Thomas Roy Peyton, excerpt from *Quest for Dignity: An Autobiography of a Negro Doctor*

Thomas Roy Peyton (1897–1968) was a prominent Los Angeles physician when he took his family to Brazil for several months in 1946 and 1947. He lived in both Rio de Janeiro and São Paulo, where he was a clinical consultant and lecturer in proctology. Peyton was born in Brooklyn and graduated from the Long Island College of Medicine in the early 1920s. He studied in Paris and London and practiced in Jamaica, Newark, and Philadelphia before moving to California in 1944.

IN RIO DE JANEIRO everyone was friendly and kind. We went to innumerable social affairs, all lavish and attended by persons of every shade of color one could imagine. We attended so many of these affairs we became wearied of the constant round. But whenever we stayed away from some function worried queries would come from Brazilian doctors the next day, each one deploring our absence. These hospitable Brazilian medicos could not understand that at, and after similar scientific gatherings

Peyton's autobiography was first published in Los Angeles by W. F. Lewis in 1950. The material reprinted here is from pp. 112, 128–29, 133–34, 138, and 146–47.

in the United States, a Negro was never allowed to participate freely. They had no idea that in North America well-meaning hosts would be literally ostracized if found responsible for inviting a Negro to a banquet or a smoker.

.   .   .

While seated alone at a table for two in the first-class diner of the train [from Rio de Janeiro to São Paulo], which was then edging its way over the mountains, another Negro entered and looked about for a seat. Single seats were vacant at several other tables where white people sat. He looked at these vacancies two or three times before glancing my way. Curious as to what he would do, I pretended unconcern. I knew what would have happened in similar circumstances on a diner in the southern area of the United States, and also knew what his probable choice would have been on a train in the northern section of my own country. There would not have been any hesitation because he would have known he was expected to sit opposite me, since I was the sole diner of color present.

But this Brazilian colored man had no such feelings. With him it was simply the matter of deciding which seat he preferred. Apparently he wanted to sit next to a white couple for that is exactly where he sat. There were no requests for curtains to be drawn to exclude him from other people, nor was he asked to move. This is the sort of freedom which made me love Brazil, a country where a person is treated as a man, no matter what his color may be.

At Mass one Sunday in Do Rosario Church on Praca Paysandy Square in the heart of downtown São Paulo, I gazed dumbfounded, with unbelieving eyes, at the congregation, which was at least 60 percent Negro. But that was not the astonishing feature! There were Negro priests and choir boys, something seldom seen in the United States, but the many holy statues in sight were of black saints, including St. Antonio Cephegero and Ste. Ephegenia! And *mirabile dictu*—A BLACK MADONNA HELD A WHITE CHILD IN HER ARMS!!! Instantly I thought to myself, what would Rankin[1] or Bilbo[2] say to this? Here, for the first time in my life, I beheld a realistic view of the heaven sought by all Christians. They envisioned it as a place where there were black as well as white saints. Apparently the incongruity of a *black* Madonna mothering her *white* child didn't bother these honest-hearted souls. The rabble-rousers like Gerald L. K. Smith[3] and his ilk probably would use this scene for a scurrilous diatribe against the evils of miscegenation.

An American, born and bred with long years of experience with the snide persecution met by every Negro, might feel doubtful that one would receive a square deal from white saints. In my native country no dark-skinned individual can be blamed for surmising that there might be more or less segregation in heaven. From birth to the day of his death, the American Negro has segregation drummed into his heart, as can be quickly learned by any northern-bred Negro if he will take a railroad or bus ride below the Mason and Dixon line. He need not go further south than Washington, D.C., to discover he no longer is a citizen with all the rights that title supposedly gives. In fact, in far too many sections of the United States, he need only walk into the first church he comes to and thus find out how little standing he has as a human being. Only in the Catholic Church have I found true equality of treatment accorded me by members and by the priests. Is it any wonder a Negro leaves one of those churches with a sense of dignity and deep spiritual reverence?

·   ·   ·

Englishmen who frequented the Jequiti [a fashionable bar and restaurant in São Paulo] usually kept to themselves, as did many of the Americans, as well as some Americanized Brazilians. A few of the latter tried to ape what they assumed to be American mannerisms and customs, even those bequeathed by Southerners who hated Negroes. This sort resulted from the infiltration of Americans just after the Civil War when members of various families among southern planters fled to Brazil to establish homes and rear their children far from the dreadful carpet-baggers, a species as greatly disliked by enlightened Negroes as by thoughtful white persons. Of course they brought the seeds of race prejudice to Brazil and attempted to cultivate these in the new land. To some extent they succeeded. Some Brazilians openly displayed a hostile attitude toward their darker countrymen, hoping to impress and please certain American friends. But on the whole, this influence remained practically inert. In Brazil no Jim Crow cars operated nor were there any laws setting up racial segregation. While darker Brazilians usually were the poorer ones, they could and did move about unrestrictedly without any feelings of inferiority. Every Brazilian, regardless of race, or creed or color of skin, seemed to enjoy the utmost freedom in every part of the country, so far as I could judge.

·   ·   ·

Next day was devoted to shopping and visits to as many places of interest as possible. Sarah was a little disappointed by the too-evident poverty of the people of color along the highways. Tom[4] and I tried to assuage her disappointment by calling attention to the air of freedom everywhere apparent. True, these people were scantily clad by American standards and certainly they had little or no cash in pocket. Yet all of them walked with dignity and a pride of bearing never seen among, and surely not characteristic of, the Negro in America. In the States there is a peculiar chip-on-the-shoulder attitude adopted by countless Negroes. They may bow their heads subserviently, but subconsciously feel a rebellion against unjust oppression. That pugnacious look is never seen among people of color in Brazil.

.   .   .

As sailing time approached,[5] friends urged me to go personally and pick up the tickets. This suggestion set up waves of doubt in my mind. After ten months of freedom in Brazil, I wondered if the steamship line would refuse us passage due to color. When Gladys[6] and I presented ourselves at the ticket office after making an appointment by telephone, my doubts were soon realized. We had understood the tickets were ready and needed only to be paid for, after which they would be given to us. But the young lady at the window stumblingly explained that some mistake had been made.

"So much confusion these days—bookings are being shuffled and reshuffled. Ships are late. Vessels are unable to sail for various reasons. There are strikes." And she "was terribly sorry, but reservations could not be honored on the 'Chinese Prince.' Maybe the next boat might have some space."

She made no mention of color, but her confusion was

telltale, as was an ostentatious search through papers and records for the missing tickets. She made several trips into an inner office searching for these vanished documents. We gave no hint we surmised her reason for being so confused.

At last the poor girl exposed her mental upset by blurting out, "I'm doing everything I can for you!"

When I asked for the manager, she replied he was out. Then I explained that I was a guest of the Brazilian National Government, that I had come to Brazil at the invitation of a government official, had spoken before the Inter-American Medical Congress, and that during our entire stay in Brazil up to this time, no prejudice due to color had been experienced. But she insisted there was absolutely no space on the "Chinese Prince." We left the steamship offices in disillusionment. However, we now determined to carry the issue to the top officials in Brazil.

A local passenger agent, a Mr. MacIntyre, who booked tourists on various Continental excursions, backed up our claim for he had helped me arrange for the reservations in the first place. Eventually the call from the booking office came. The sugary-voiced clerk informed that our tickets were waiting. Would we "kindly come in and pick them up?" We certainly would, and I did!

The ship's sailing was delayed at Santos for some extra cargo, so I took a run over there to see what our seventeen-day home looked like. We boarded the ship and asked the steward to show us the assigned cabin called for by our tickets. He hastened to the purser's office and brought back the passenger list.

"Oh, yes," he mused, "Doctor, you have Cabin No. 9. Men and women assigned to separate cabins, you know, to conserve space and regardless of relationships. Your wife and daughter will be in Cabin 4, and your son has Cabin 8."

We had reserved a single cabin for the family and I suggested as much. But he only replied, "Sorry, passage to the States is difficult these days. This isn't a passenger ship, anyhow. I'll see what I can do for you."

Next day, with heavy hearts, we climbed aboard and began a desultory search for the three different cabins. The steward, met the day before, suddenly appeared, a big grin on his face, explaining, "Your family will occupy Stateroom No. 11." We entered it and had a hearty laugh *en famille*. Sometimes it *is* nice to be a Negro! Then you can enjoy the privacy of a single cabin while white families are separated into several cabins. But these experiences as the only passengers of color were just beginning, as we speedily learned.

When the ship sailed from Brazil we had feelings of deep regret and genuine gratitude for the happiness its hospitable shores had given us. Away from land we soon sensed an atmosphere of racial tension. Our fellow passengers politely ignored us, except for some Jewish people returning from Argentina.

NOTES

1. John E. Rankin was a Mississippi congressman (1921–53) known for his anti-black views.
2. Theodore G. Bilbo was a controversial, demagogic Mississippi politician who served in the Senate from 1935 until his death in 1947. He was a leader of those who sought to undercut the position of blacks, immigrants, and labor unions.

3. Smith was a northern-born clergyman who moved to Louisiana in 1928 where he became a key supporter of Governor Huey P. Long. After Long's assassination in 1935 he became active in various anti–New Deal and anti-black, anti-Catholic, anti-Jewish groups seeking a "white, Christian America."

4. Thomas Griffin, a Los Angeles dentist, and his wife, Sarah, visited the Peytons in Rio.

5. The author does not give the date or month of his departure from Brazil in 1947.

6. The author's wife.

19.

George S. Schuyler, "Brazilian Color Bias Growing More Rampant"

George S. Schuyler (1895–1977), associate editor of the Pittsburgh Courier *from 1942 to 1964, was sent on a six-week tour of Brazil and several other Latin American republics in the summer of 1948. He wrote a number of feature articles based on his experiences. His views about race in Latin America were summarized in "Color Lines in Latin America,"* Negro Digest *7 (May 1949), 52–57, and in his autobiography,* Black and Conservative *(New Rochelle, N.Y., 1966), 289–315.*

Bar U.S. Woman

BOTH COLORED and white people are still talking about the refusal of the swank Hotel Serrado to honor the reservation of Dr. Irene Diggs,[1] noted U.S. scholar, because she was discovered to be a Negro. That was only a year ago, and while the management hastened to make amends to the outraged Rio de Janeiro public by giving a local

From the *Pittsburgh Courier*, September 4, 1948. Reprinted by permission of the New Pittsburgh Courier Publishing Co., Pittsburgh, Pennsylvania.

Negro a week's free lodging in a palatial suite, the Diggs incident is still cited as a horrible example of the trend to lily-whitism.

The writer had an eye-opening experience at another exclusive hotel, The Gloria, also in Rio. As soon as the taxicab drove up to the entrance and it was observed that a black man was getting out with his luggage, two bellboys rushed out crying in broken English, "Got reservation? Got reservation?" This incident was not regarded as significant at the time, but after sitting in the lobby for an half hour waiting for a telephone call and observing incoming guests, it was noted that none was asked by the bellboys, "Got reservation?" All of them were white.

Swank Schools Bar

Pursuing information on this paradoxical situation, it was learned that distinguishable Negroes are a rarity in the military, naval and air corps academies; that a number of private schools would not dream of having an obviously Negro student, and that the Fundação Rio Branco, which prepares young men for diplomatic careers, has never had any more Negroes than the University of Mississippi, where colored students are equally persona non grata.

No discernible Negroes were observed drinking at tables in the very exclusive bars along Rio's Copacabana and Avenida Atlântico, nor in comparable places in downtown areas. Some Negroes say they cannot be served there. The writer was served in several such places, but this was scarcely a real test because he was in the company of whites.

It is further reported on good authority that the various religious orders will not accept Negroes except as lay members. However, there are said to be a considerable number of Negro and Negroid priests and nuns scattered over the country, although whether there are many more than in the United States is doubtful.

Fought Football Bias

It is pointed out by embittered blacks that a strenuous fight had to be waged to get Negroes admitted to the football (soccer) clubs of Rio de Janeiro. It is a matter of record that in April, 1944, business men with establishments in the famous Paulista Triangulo in São Paulo, Brazil's Chicago, petitioned the government to stop colored workers from passing through that exclusive shopping area.

About the same time colored recreational clubs located in that section were pointedly invited to depart. Coupled with the almost total absence of Negroes from behind the counters of commercial and banking establishments, as observed in Rio, Salvador, Recife and Belém, this all adds up to a rather serious color bar. . . .

"White" States

The consensus of opinion is that in the predominantly white states of São Paulo, Rio Grande do Sul and Santa Catarina, anti-Negro prejudice is growing and color discrimination is rife. These are the southern states into which there has been much European immigration, largely from Italy and Germany. Most of Brazil's Negroes are in the states of Bahia and Minas Gerais, and the Federal Department of Rio de Janeiro.

One might be inclined to think the Negroes were exaggerating, were it not for the hard fact that they have found it necessary to establish defense organizations like Frente Negra Brasileira and União Dos Homens De Côr Dos Estados Unidos Do Brasil (Union of Men of Color of the U.S. of Brazil) which are actively fighting bias.

Strong Organization

The latter organization is the strongest. It is a benefit society founded January 3, 1943, by its president, Dr. João C. Alves, in Pôrto Alegre, State of Rio Grande do Sul. Dr. Alves is also managing editor of its official organ *União* (Union), "a non-political and independent weekly" published in São Paulo. Its statement of purpose is enlightening:

"Our society aims to raise the economic and intellectual level of all persons of color throughout the nation in order to make it possible for them to enter into the social and administrative life of the country in every sector of its activity, without regard to race, so that persons of color will be accepted with the whites on conditions of equality."

The organization is interracial in membership, advocates cooperative residences for single people of both races in all State capitals, establishment of old folk's homes, elimination of illiteracy and abolition of slums, most of which are predominantly populated by poor Negroes.

In its issue of July 8, 1948, *Union* asserts editorially: "Although it may seem absurd and incomprehensible, color prejudice has greatly increased in Brazil during the past thirteen years."

Theatre Jim Crow

Another shock is to discover that jim crow rules the Brazilian theatre so thoroughly. If and when permitted on the stage, the Negro's role is that of clown, blackguard or Uncle Tom (Pai João). Sometimes beautiful mulatto girls are hired to sing and dance half-naked at stage shows. The serious stage is strictly for whites.

It is because of this deplorable situation that Abdias do Nascimento, a São Paulo ex-soldier, and Aguinaldo Camargo, whom the critic Eugene Rassencourt has called "Brazil's Finest Actor," founded in 1944, the Teatro Experimental do Negro (Negro Experimental Theater). Their dual objective is to furnish a medium through which Negro dramatic talent may be brought to the front and to raise the cultural and social status of the Brazilian Negro.

As Abdias has put it, "What we hope to accomplish with the Negro Experimental Theater, the Afro-Brazilian Orchestra, and the Afro-Brazilian Cultural Center is to give some measure of evaluation to the colored people, to try and awake in them new hopes and the stimulus to seek a better pattern of living."

Fine Talent

The Negro Experimental Theater which has a branch in São Paulo and hopes to have branches throughout Brazil some day, has already developed some fine talent such as Ruth de Souza, the nation's leading Negro actress. She has appeared in almost all the plays the group has produced. Among them being "O Filho Pródigo," "Palmares" (with the Student's Theater), "The Emperor Jones" and "All God's Chillun Got Wings."

Unfortunately the group works under great difficulties such as lack of money and a theater. They move around from one place to another wherever a house is vacant and sometimes have no place to rehearse. It costs them $500 to launch a production and such money is hard to come by even though the effort has been highly praised and publicized.

Negro Held Inferior

It seems clear that the Negro is held to be inferior not only by the whites and near-whites but, tragically, by the blacks themselves. The latter think they have improved their status if they can marry someone lighter than themselves, preferably a white person; and because of the peculiar historical background here, there is no opposition to and little prejudice against such marriages.

Eugene Rassencourt, the Chicago expatriate writer who is a keen observer of the color question here and a good friend of the Negroes, holds that: "Brazil today is run, or at least regulated, by a white minority, the U.S. by a white majority."

Miscegenation Advances

It is for this reason that racial intermarriage is not frowned upon by the Brazilian whites since traditionally they had to augment their small numbers by socially admitting near-whites. The process of miscegenation has gone so far now that there are less unmixed colored folk in Brazil than you will find in the U.S.A.

There is a white feeling the Negroes must "prove" their equality. The whites don't hate them, just pity them;

and have a strong prejudice against associating with them on terms of equality. Even the white men with Negro or mulatto mistresses will not be seen publicly with them, it is said.

Negro Equals Poverty

Brazilian society is without a middle class, so the gulf between the rich and the poor is more obvious than elsewhere—and it is some gulf. The Negro slaves were emancipated as late as May 13, 1888, and most of them have advanced little farther than they were then. Thus they fall naturally into the lowest part of the lower class economically.

There are plenty of whites as poor, illiterate and unhealthy as the poorest Negroes, but if they can acquire some money, they can escape and be accepted into the white ruling class. Rarely is this true in the case of the successful black man.

Resent Name "Negro"

There are many prominent men of obviously Negro ancestry who have "arrived," but most of them do not want to be identified in any way with the Negro. And unless they are dark brown or endowed with other African features, they resent being called Negroes.

The Mayor of São Paulo is what we would call a Negro. So is Sen. Melo Vianna, vice president of the Brazilian Senate. So is Octavio Mangabeira, Governor of Bahia. So is the professor of law at the University of São Paulo (a wealthy corporation attorney) and many others of light skin, but they would regard it as libelous to be called

Negroes. In Salvador, Recife, São Paulo, Belém, Belo Horizonte and smaller places, there are some successful men of color but they have the same attitude, and perhaps they can scarcely be blamed.

Camaraderie

Little of the foregoing is immediately apparent to the eye of the transient visitor. What he sees is (to a U.S.A. citizen) a revelation. He sees interracial camaraderie on every hand. Here are black and white walking arm in arm.

Here are colored and white bathers sitting and chatting on the Praça Paris sea wall. Here is an attractive, well-dressed white girl on the Avenida Rio Branco chatting amiably with a young brown-skinned gallant. Here a white man and a brown man meet on a prominent street embracing each other affectionately in the Brazilian manner. Here is a young white student admitting that he prefers the pretty mulatto girls of Salvador to all the blondes in the world, and quite serious about it.

Here is a free association between all colors that is astonishing and reassuring. It shows that the masses of Brazilians do not share the social snobbery of the top whites. On beaches, in bars, in movies and on the street chromatic democracy seems to prevail.

In most public places frequented by the generality from eight to eighty, the color line seems as remote as Mars. In this connection Brazil is a mass of contradictions, just like the U.S.A., so that anything anybody says about interracial relations, good or bad, is apt to be true. Racism is unquestionably here but only the most discerning can see it at first glance.

Widely Employed

The Brazilian colored folk are more widely employed than their U.S.A. brethren. You will find them among the skilled workers on all construction jobs, in the fire departments of the various cities, in all the police forces, in the Army and Navy, cleaning streets, driving trucks, in the symphony orchestra, in all dance hall bands, in all positions on buses and street cars, as firemen and engineers on the railroads, as public school teachers, here and there as clerks in hotels and bookkeepers. In Federal and State offices many colored people are clerks and hold responsible positions. . . .

Horrible Housing

With low wages and inflation prices, it is understandable that the housing of the masses, especially in the large cities is pretty bad. In Rio there are miles of ultra-modern skyscraper apartment houses along fine boulevards but rentals are out of the masses' reach. So the poor live in back alleys, far out in the suburbs or in the 119 favelas, or squatter settlements, fastened to the steep sugarloaf mountains of the capital.

These latter settlements have to be seen to be believed. Constructed of all sorts of scrap, these slums are without electric lights, running water or sewers. The odor of laundry water and sewage hangs over them, and to climb to the top of one of them is an exhausting ordeal which enhances one's respect for the poor women who scramble up these forty and fifty-degree grades with gasoline cans full of water on their heads two or three times a day. All colors and races are represented here where rent is free, but colored people predominate.

In cities like Salvador, São Paulo, Recife and Belém, the masses live in smelly tenements which seemingly were old when George Washington was young, and they are packed like sardines.

Illiteracy and Disease

Understanding this situation, it is not surprising that illiteracy and disease are rife. There are the usual regulations, laws and provisions on paper about compulsory education, but the hard fact is that Brazil is an illiterate country.

In Rio the illiteracy rate is around 75 percent. In the State of Pará it is about 80 percent. In the City of Salvador, with a population of 322,830 as of 1936, the 1940 population of school age was 49,239, and in 1947 there were 8,600 in public and 9,000 in private schools.

In all Brazil with its 45,000,000 population, there are 3,824,525 elementary, intermediate and high school pupils in public and private schools, and a total of 122,871 teachers, or about twice the number of Negro teachers in the United States. The college population is under 20,000 whereas one-third that number of Negroes here are graduated from college annually from a total colored population of 14,000,000.

Education Level

In short, Brazilian education for all colors seems to be about on the level of Negro education in the U.S.A. During the school year the streets swarm with children. In Rio only one-third are ever in school.

Primary teachers begin at about $35 a month on the average, with the first raise after two years. A principal can work his way up to $200 or $250 a month. The percentage of men teachers is small. It is estimated that 10 percent of the teachers are blacks and around 50 percent mulattoes, but there are understandably no statistics on this.

Health Problem

By common agreement the health of most Brazilians is pretty bad. [The] worst affliction is tuberculosis, thanks to malnutrition from which two-thirds of the population suffers. There are also thirty-eight leper colonies in Brazil and 138 leper protection societies.

While yellow fever has been virtually eliminated, malaria, bubonic plague, venereal disease and endemic goitre are widespread and constitute a grave menace which the Government is striving manfully to control through its 1,226 public and 1,144 private hospitals and infirmaries. There is also a Social Welfare Nutrition Service which tries to teach the people to eat better and operates a few low-cost cafeterias with health menus in the larger cities.

Since colored people constitute the lowest group, socially and economically, these conditions make clear why their status is what it is.

Rich Country

Brazil is bigger than the United States and it would take years to cover all of it. It is potentially very rich but requires much capital to develop it so that the masses can benefit from these great natural endowments. Here and there are a few intelligent and enterprising Negroes from the U.S.A. who have made good, and others who have a trade or profession can do likewise—if they are willing to go there with a little capital, work hard, become citizens and marry Brazilians. It is extremely difficult for aliens to get work permits.

Brazilian colored folk have practically no businesses, not even in Rio de Janeiro where nearly a half million of them reside. The same is true in the other cities, with the exception of a private school or a little shop. There are many in the taxicab business in Rio and some were seen driving private buses licensed by the city to carry passengers. Whether these vehicles were owned by them could not be ascertained.

White-Collar Jobs

The educated Negroes seem to prefer the white-collar professions to entering business. This is in accordance with Latin American tradition, but quite naturally it leaves them unrepresented in the fields which really count most in modern civilization. They will have to change direction or else stay behind the march of progress.

Politically, Brazilian Negroes are almost nil. Save for teaching jobs, police, firemen, Government clerks and minor officials, they have no share in Government. There is one obvious Negro in Congress, but there seem to be no judges or district attorneys, and of course, there is none in the diplomatic service. Of course they do not vote as Negroes but as Brazilians, when they vote at all. . . .

Behind U.S. Standard

Brazil is a country which in general is about at the place where the United States of America was fifty years ago, and it will take a long time for the country as a whole to reach our standard of living. Of course a small, wealthy white minority lives better than many of our rich, but for the masses an automobile and an electric refrigerator will long be out of the question. Negroes in Mississippi own more of both than all the colored people in all Latin America.

It is noteworthy that only 1,200,000 houses in all Brazil have electric lights. These things are not the sole criteria of progress but they are a gauge in this modern world.

As for the colored people, one can close with no better statement than that of the brilliant Abdias do Nascimento:

> It is said that in Brazil there is no race problem for the colored man. An effort is made to scatter far and wide before the winds of propaganda the idea that here in Brazil the Negro has found his paradise where he may enjoy equal rights with other men. Don't believe this . . . If the race drama here does not take the form of bellicosity and physical clashes, that does not mean that it does not exist. It is something that exists psychologically for a great part of the population, this veiled racial discrimination, mystified among the propositions of a constitution which defines all men equal before the law.

NOTE

1. Irene Diggs is an anthropologist best known for research on Afro-Latin American culture and the African diaspora. She

studied at the University of Minnesota and at Atlanta University, where she worked as W.E.B. Du Bois's research assistant from 1932 to 1943. She received her Ph.D. from the University of Havana in 1944 and taught at Morgan State College in Baltimore, Maryland, until her retirement in 1976.

20.
Lorenzo D. Turner, "The Negro in Brazil"

> *Lorenzo Dow Turner (1895–1972) was a linguist who specialized in the study of African cultural survivals in the New World. He was educated at Howard University, Harvard, and the University of Chicago, where he received a Ph.D. in English in 1926. He taught at Howard University, Fisk University, and Roosevelt University. His best-known work was* Africanisms in the Gullah Dialect *(1949). The research referred to in this article was done while the author was a Rosenwald Fellow in Brazil, 1940–41. His only other published essay on Brazil was "Some Contacts of Brazilian Ex-Slaves with Nigeria, West Africa,"* Journal of Negro History *27 (January 1942), 55–67. Both essays reflect his interest in the issue of African cultural survivals in the Americas.*

PROBABLY VERY FEW persons in the United States are aware of the tremendous influence which Africans have exerted upon the culture of Brazil. Some historians have estimated that between the middle of the sixteenth century and the middle of the nineteenth from ten to twelve

From the *Chicago Jewish Forum* 15 (Summer 1957), 232–36.

million Africans were imported to Brazil as slaves. It is impossible for one to be certain, however, even of an approximate number, because when slavery was abolished in Brazil in 1888 the government ordered all documents and records relating to slavery to be destroyed. Though this order was not strictly carried out in many sections of the country, the documents that remain are not sufficient to give a complete picture of slavery in Brazil. As late as the first quarter of the nineteenth century, however, there were three times as many Negroes there as Europeans. . . .

Many of these Africans, like many of those who came to the United States, were from the upper socio-economic strata of African societies, including kings, princes, chiefs of tribes, priests, military specialists, and other such groups. Inter-tribal wars in Africa frequently resulted in the imprisonment of the conquered rulers, together with all of their followers, and subsequently in their being sold to white slave-traders and being brought to the New World. The slaves in Brazil, however, enjoyed many advantages that were denied their brothers in the United States, the British West Indies, and the French possessions in the Caribbean. For example, manumission for the Brazilian slave was comparatively easy; and once free, he had all of the rights and privileges of any other citizen of the country. Unlike the status of a child born in the United States of a slave mother and a white father, the child so born in Brazil took the status of the father, and thus was born free. Again, when two slave parents had ten children, the entire family was automatically free. Moreover, throughout the long period of slavery in Brazil there was a government official, known as the protector of slaves, who looked after the welfare of slaves treated with cruelty and who had the authority to deprive the owners of slaves so treated. The

Brazilian law also provided that slaves should enjoy special privileges on 85 (in some states 104) days out of every year. On these days they could earn enough money to buy their freedom and their owners were compelled to permit them to do so at a price not higher than that at which they had been purchased. There were still other provisions whereby Brazilian slaves could obtain their freedom. In these ways thousands of slaves became free. So extensive, in fact, was manumission that by 1888, when slavery was abolished in Brazil, a large majority of the Negroes were already free and were participating actively in all phases of Brazilian life.

As a further indication of the Brazilian's attitude toward slavery and the Negro, as compared with that of slaveholders in some other countries, it should be noted that there was no civil war in Brazil resulting from the movement to abolish slavery, as occurred in the United States; nor were the former slaveholders reimbursed by the government for surrendering their slaves, as was done in the British territories. . . .

African religious cult practices, which have never been seriously interfered with in Brazil, have been the most fruitful source of African survivals in the New World. In the cult communities of Bahia and other states of Northeastern Brazil, native African religious ceremonies are basically the same as they were when brought to Brazil during the period of slavery. In these communities one can still see authentic African dances, costumes, and artifacts and hear authentic African drum rhythms, songs, chants, prayers, and stories. From these African cult communities both religious and secular songs and dances, as well as other elements of African culture, have spread throughout Brazil and far beyond its borders.

A few years ago the present writer brought back from Northeastern Brazil approximately six hundred twelve-inch phonograph records which he made principally in these cult communities. The entire contents of these records are African and represent at least five West African languages. Many of the ex-slaves and their descendants still speak some of the African languages, notably Yoruba, Ewe, Fon, and Kimbundu, and according to this writer's own findings several thousand African words have become a permanent part of the vocabulary of Brazilian Portuguese.

Many of the most famous Brazilian musicians . . . owe their fame largely to their use of African themes and melodies. . . . On the faculties of conservatories of music in Brazil, in orchestras and bands, and in the philharmonic societies, the Negro has long been well represented, and in many sections of the country he practically dominates the radio stations as a singer and musician. Several African musical instruments, such as the ilú (a drum), the cuica, the agogô (an iron gong), the birambau (a musical bow), the chequerê (a rattle), the chocalho (a rattle), and others are well known in Brazil.

In Brazilian sculpture, painting, and architecture the Negro has also distinguished himself. Among the early artists in these fields are Aleijadinho (1730–1813), whose productions adorn many of the most famous churches and parks in Brazil. One of the distinguished modern artists of Brazil is Santa Rosa, a mulatto, who has been especially active as a scenic painter and an illustrator of books and periodicals.

Like the Negro in the United States, the Brazilian Negro has made a significant contribution to the folk tale of the New World. Many ex-slaves and their descendants still tell these tales not only in Portuguese but also in the African languages; and Negro themes have been the chief inspiration of many leading writers of Brazil.

In the field of science, several Brazilian Negroes have become famous. André Rebouças, an able mathematician and engineer, was in charge of the construction of the Rio de Janeiro Customs House and prepared plans for the Rio docks. He was an outstanding authority on water power and utilization. During the war with Paraguay he invented a torpedo for the use of the navy and gave advice on certain technical aspects of the campaign. Theodoro Sampaio was not only a noted engineer but also an authority on Tupi, an Indian language. In the field of medicine, especially psychiatry, Juliano Moreira, who died a few years ago, achieved great distinction. He was Director General of the Hospital for the Insane in Rio de Janeiro and honorary professor of the Faculty of Medicine in Bahia.

Like the Negro soldier in the United States, the Brazilian Negro has shown great skill and courage on the battlefield. The late Arthur Ramos says that the "military history of Brazil, from the colonization to the present time, must give pre-eminence to the contributions of men of the Negro race." At one time the proportion of Negroes to whites in the Brazilian army was three to one. Throughout the sixteenth century the Negro was the principal element in the conquest of Brazil. In the wars between the Dutch and the Portuguese in Brazil in the seventeenth century, in the war between Brazil and Paraguay in the nineteenth, and in all later conflicts, Negroes were the chief participants.

The Brazilian Negro also has reached the highest positions in the political life of the nation, both in the states and in the federal government. One of Brazil's presidents, Nilo Peçanho, was of Negro ancestry. He had served in the first Congress of the Republic, then in the Senate, then as vice-president, and in June, 1909, was elected president of Brazil. He served until November, 1910. In 1912, he was re-elected to the Senate, and later became president of the State of Rio de Janeiro. He died in 1924.

Since the emancipation of the slaves the Negro has participated fully in the social and family life of Brazil. There is no law prohibiting such participation or the exercise of any legitimate function of the citizen. Racial friction in Brazil is at a minimum. In fact, one is scarcely aware of one's color there. The terms for black, brown, white, etc. are used primarily for purposes of identification. Gilberto Freyre, a distinguished Brazilian scholar, has emphasized the fact that though Brazil is mainly Portuguese in its origins and Catholic of the Latin variety, its background is not purely European, but also African; not purely Christian, but also Jewish and Mohammedan. "Hereditarily predisposed to a life in the tropics by a long tropical habitat, it was the Semitic element," he says, "mobile and adaptable as no other, that was to confer upon the Portuguese colonizer of Brazil some of the chief physical and psychic conditions for success and for resistance—including that economic realism which from an early date tended to correct the excesses of the military and religious spirit in the formation of Brazilian society." He says further that the Christianity of the Portuguese and of their colonizers in Brazil became more human as a result of contact with the religion of Mohammad and other non-Christian religions both in the Iberian Peninsula and in Brazil. "It is a Christianity in which the Infant Jesus is identified with Cupid, and the Virgin Mary and the saints with the concerns of procreation and love rather than with chastity and asceticism." The general result of this long contact of both the

Spanish and Portuguese peoples with these varied ethnic and religious groups has been one of "integration, or balance of contending elements, rather than of segregation, or sharp differentiation, of any of them or violent conflicts between them."

PART III

The Myth Rejected (1965–)

AFRICAN-AMERICAN responses to Brazil—and to the rest of the world—have always been in large part a reflection of domestic events. At no time has this been more apparent than since the mid-1960s and 1970s.[1]

A number of developments in American society, and within the black community in particular, contributed to the reexamination of race relations in Brazil: the heated debates over Stanley Elkins's thesis that under Anglo-American slavery Africans became Sambos;[2] a widespread loss of confidence in the ability or desire of whites to create significant changes in black–white relations; and the conflicts among black Americans that accompanied the demise of the civil rights movement. Implicit in Elkins's work and in much of that by other white scholars was the notion that people of African ancestry in Brazil were better off than their cousins in the North and that these differences had their origins in disparate slave systems. The extensive social and biological mixture of the races in Brazil and the absence of overt segregation and violence seemed to validate the gradualistic, nonviolent, and integrationist approach of the civil rights movement in the 1950s and early 1960s. As the racial environment in the United States became more heated in the late 1960s and as the ideology and tactics of Martin Luther King, Jr., came under ever-sharper criticism by younger, more nationalistic and impatient black Americans, the Brazilian experience was reexamined. In a time of "Black Power" and "Black Is Beautiful," Brazil became less and less appealing. Indeed, the relative absence of racial consciousness and organization in Brazil and the emphasis on whitening were seen as evils or traps to be avoided, not as features worthy of emulation.

Instead of a racial eldorado, Brazil increasingly appeared to be a runaround or worse for people of color. Black American critics warned that the belief that the races lived together in peace and harmony in Brazil was both false and dangerous. The myth of the racial paradise, they insisted, stifled black pride and power in Brazil and reinforced the propensity of liberal whites at home to pursue gradualistic, assimilationist, and colorblind policies.

In addition to being more nationalistic in outlook, black North American intellectuals since the mid-1960s have paid more attention to the role of social class in perpetuating the subordinate status of African Americans. These scholars tend to see fewer differences in the systems of social stratification in Brazil and in the United States. Class oppression, they note, goes hand-in-hand with racial oppression in Brazil as well as in the United States. This perspective undercuts the assertion traditionally advanced by Brazilian defenders of the myth of the social democracy, that class barriers—poverty and lack of education in particular—account for the gap between Euro- and Afro-Brazilians.

The selections included in Part III—and others written since the mid-1960s[3]—are as consistent in their rejection of the traditional view of Brazilian society as those from the first third of the century were in support of the image. The essays convey the continuing importance of Afro-Latin America to blacks in the United States. Brazil, each author seems to say, contains a message for Americans, albeit one very different from that found there a half-century before. The lessons of Brazil are many: that black Americans are not alone; that people of African descent in the New World share a common background and face similar challenges; that it is important to affirm one's biological and cultural heritage and resist pressures toward "whitening"; and, above all, that racial oppression takes many forms.

Notes

1. The shift in African-American attitudes regarding Brazil is traced more fully in David J. Hellwig, "Racial Paradise or Run-around? Afro–North American Views of Race Relations in Brazil," *American Studies* 31 (Fall 1990), 43–60.

2. Stanley Elkins, *Slavery: A Problem in American Institutional and Intellectual Life* (New York, 1959); Ann J. Lane, ed., *The Debate Over "Slavery": Stanley Elkins and His Critics* (Urbana, 1971).

3. The first two essays in this section were published in early 1970, as was Ann Cook's "Black Pride—Some Contradictions," *Negro Digest* 19 (January 1970), 40–42, and thus they were formulated in the late 1960s. An editorial in the *Negro Digest* 17 (September/October 1968), 49–51, "The Coming Revolution in Brazil," also sharply rejected the notion of the racial paradise. For other assessments of Brazil written during the past two decades, see Michael Mitchell, "Racial Consciousness and the Political Attitudes and Behavior of Blacks in São Paulo, Brazil" (Ph.D. diss., Indiana University, 1977); the essays by Pierre-Michel Fontaine, J. Michael Turner, and Michael Mitchell in Pierre-Michel Fontaine, ed., *Race, Class and Power in Brazil* (Los Angeles, 1985); and I. K. Sundiata, "Late Twentieth Century Patterns of Race Relations in Brazil and the United States," *Phylon* 48 (March 1987), 62–76. For a rare post-1965 statement affirming the traditional view of race relations in Brazil, see Melvin Boozer, "Developing Human Communities: A Brazilian Experience," *The Crisis* 78 (November 1971), 293–97.

21.
Angela M. Gilliam, "From Roxbury to Rio—and Back in a Hurry"

Angela M. Gilliam is an anthropologist who currently teaches at Evergreen State College. Her 1975 dissertation at Union Graduate School was entitled "Language Attitudes, Ethnicity and Class in São Paulo and Salvador da Bahia (Brazil)." Her views on race relations in Brazil are further developed in "Black and White in Latin America," Présence Africaine 92 (Paris, 1974), 161–73.

ONE OF THE greatest myths propagated throughout the world is that representing Brazil as a place of supreme racial harmony—the solution, as it were, to the world's racial crisis. The ancillary mythology in this regard is that slavery under Portuguese rule was somewhat of a lark, while being a slave in Anglo-Saxon territory was

From the *Journal of Black Poetry* I (Winter-Spring 1970), 8–12. Reprinted by permission of the author. This article was originally directed to a broad cross-section of the black community. It was written during a period in which the author was still influenced by black nationalism—a U.S. variant of Pan-Africanist thought. The emergence in the 1970s of Africans in both Mozambique and Angola who received financial and political support from pro-apartheid forces caused many African Americans to reevaluate their politics during the wars for independence in these former Portuguese colonies. For Gilliam, the experience of teaching at the University of Coimbra in Portugal during this period contributed to a permanent ideological shift toward global egalitarianism.

more difficult. A slave is a slave is a slave. It makes no difference whether or not a concentration camp has the name of "relocation center" (nomenclature for the American concentration camps for the Japanese-Americans during World War II), reservation, or ghetto. The problems and solutions do not change because of title, location or nationality.

Portugal was the first country to send slavers into Africa and it is still in the Homeland, yet many black people in this country have been deluded into thinking that the Portuguese are somewhat more humane than Anglo-Saxons in their treatment of black people in this hemisphere. Many of the reasons for this are due to the cloudy perceptions and questionable orientations of blacks who have traveled to Brazil and then passed on their interpretations in the forms of sociological treatises or magazine articles.

This brings me to one of the questions we want to face here. Why do people assume that legalized physical oppression is perforce more damaging than sub-rosa psychological cultural oppression? In both instances, a people and what they represent as humans are destroyed.

There were no lynchings in Brazil as we know them. Yet in daily life one hears the most demeaning statements about *blackness* that can be heard anywhere.

To best exemplify this, I should like to share some of my eye-opening experiences in Brazil.

Every day I received startling inputs that affected me in much the same way as do those quasi-blinding strobe light shows mixed with white electronic music. It took a while to muster up my conscious forces. I already knew that as a black person leaving this country my so-called status automatically changed, but I wasn't prepared for my looking and seeming so Brazilian that I would be accused of trying to "pass as a foreigner." In Brazil, blacks and so-called whites (we'll get to *that* later) both spoke openly of the national desire to "cleanse the blood" (limpar o sangue) and "improve the race" (melhorar a raça). This *always* means "lightening" the population. Once, at a social gathering, someone was describing another as being tall, blonde, etc. Someone else responded disparagingly, "Blonde nothing, she's a 'sarará'." "Sarará" is what we would call "mariney"—a black person with light skin, light brown hair, and sometimes blue, green or gray eyes (also Brazilian term for albino). In another instance, I heard someone who looked somewhat like H. Rap Brown[1] with short hair say he didn't like attending a certain theatre because "a negrada vai la" ("That's a 'nigra' hang-out")—and this to a group of whites!

Perhaps the most shocking experience came when I learned a rhyme that reminded me of "If you're black, stay back" et al., only worse. "A black woman to work, a white woman to marry and a 'mulata' (meaning brown-skinned woman) to screw." That just about sums up where Brazil is at, in terms of blackness as an operational concept.

Paradoxically, no country has purer pockets of African culture. The state of Bahia, according to even the statistics (which are always "lighter") is about 80 percent black. Yoruba words drift in and out of everybody's conversation naturally. According to Glauber Rocha, director of the prize-winning film, "Black God, White Devil," the true history and sociology of Brazil are found in the music written by black "samba" composers in Rio de Janeiro.

The religion is also strongly African—so much so that a "babalorixá"[2] from Bahia was able to use Bahian ritual Yoruba to communicate in Nigeria. Brazil's national dish is—get ready for this—"feijoada," or, beans cooked with a pig foot, pigtail, side of bacon, hamhocks, dried beef and served with rice and collard greens. I wish I could convey to you all the expressions I get from Brazilian "embassy wives" in New York who complain about not being able to get fresh "couve mineira" (collards) and I tell them they have got to go to Harlem because that's a black food.

Which brings us to the definition of "black" in Brazil. It's confusing—no doubt about it. It is a color, with money or lack of it, education and social class as *supplementary* elements in the definition thereof. But color is still the definitive indicator, all rumors to the contrary notwithstanding. Pelé, the world's highest paid athlete, will always be black. His daughter, however, will probably be classified as white (Pelé's wife is an Italo-Brazilian) especially if she one day marries a white man, which is likely, given that "cleansing the blood" orientation that Pelé will no doubt pass on.

Someone at Rio police headquarters once told me that, being a foreigner, I could not be classified as black. In some areas of Brazil, one can change one's race by changing jobs. Anthropologists tell of a former mailboat operator along the Amazon River who became white upon being elected mayor of his town. How? Because in the words of one of the townspeople, "It's simple, we would never have a black mayor!"

Now here is where the interpretations of E. Franklin Frazier and Era Bell Thompson[3] go awry. They hear something like the latter story and feel there is more mobility and/or equity for the black man in Brazil as a result. But what is really being touched upon here? Black is a negative so Brazilians would prefer to change the mayor's description to a positive—white. It also means that American blacks traveling to Brazil from a higher standard of living, and who therefore have more clothes, education, and other accouterments of Doris Day–Rock Hudson movies, are afforded better treatment than their Brazilian counterparts. The internalized decadence that permits someone to subsequently interpret this special consideration as being generic to *all* Brazilian blacks is a rationalization for *permitting and enjoying such special treatment, and is European individualism in its most pathological form.* It further suggests that the aforementioned writers felt agreement with the Brazilian goal of eliminating vestiges of blackness.

There are roughly forty million blacks in Brazil—40 percent of the population. Most of the forty million look like West Africans. The Portuguese quite cleverly fomented and/or used their sperm to create splinter groups, all with different names to eliminate identification with one another, and expected different behavior from and extended different justice to each group, so that a large united group would never take power even though non-whites outnumbered whites. Mulattoes do not want to marry black unless they represent more money. "Cafusos" (a person of black and Amerindian heritage) and Amerindians were used to hunt runaway slaves; a dark person with straight hair has more "market value" than a person who is lighter with kinky hair, etc. To further explain these insidious classifications, the following persons would be thusly categorized:

Kathleen Cleaver	white (with hair straightened)
Malcolm X	mulato sarará
Mrs. Martin L. King	mulato
Dr. Martin Luther King	black (or mulato if he wore a suit and tie)
Harry Belafonte	mulato
Lena Horne	white

Lola Falana	cafusa
Percy Sutton	white
Adam C. Powell	white
Sydney Poitier	black
Huey P. Newton	white (if he has the trappings of the rich)
Robert Macbeth	white

What this "classification" indicates is the confusing and varying nature of racial categorization in Brazil. In the large cities of the south, we can see the tragic scramblings of "Lola Falana" types using their beauty to get Italo-Brazilian husbands for example, so that their children will be considered white. The difference between the U.S. and Brazil, then, is this: In Brazil the phenotype (the visible physical characteristics) is the determinant of race, while in the U.S. it is the genotype (the invisible heritage in its entirety).

Looking at this, then, in contemporary Pan-African terms, I would contend that American blacks, by virtue of the imposed historical definition of *who* is or is not black, may have more advantages. That is, the identifiable (by virtue of color and/or culture) black in this country has potential for family/group unity and common goals far exceeding that which is possible in Brazil. The only possible black movement in Brazil will be due to "outside agitation" which forces the 30 percent of Brazilian population that does not see itself as black (but is indeed *African* in culture) into a confrontation with the 40 percent black population as to which direction the "cleansing of the blood" is going to take—Africanization or Europeanization. Mind you, all 80 percent would clearly be black in this country, as native born Americans. For purposes of this discussion, the rest of the 15 percent remaining do not count.[4] The runaway Nazis, Italians, Nisei [second-generation Brazilians of Japanese descent] and Lebanese who make up part of the southern region of Brazil have most of the economic power, but the major battle at this point is *conscious* cultural direction. And the most important, a vital heritage of African values and African resistance is part of Brazil. The unconscious African values have remained imbedded in all Brazilians. The heritage of Palmares is what has to be revived consciously. In 1500, the Portuguese arrived in Brazil; in 1530, the first Africans arrived as slaves; in 1600 a major slave rebellion occurred that resulted in the development of a Republic called Palmares. It consisted of a group of towns that related to the land in the African tradition and which was so successful agriculturally that the republic traded goods for guns with neighboring landlords. When this was checked out by the Portuguese, we see the commencement of the triumvirate of power that still controls Latin America. The military, church and landlords united to successfully destroy the Republic in 1696 after 27 prior military attempts. And there were other glorious traditions set by black slaves in Brazil. Often they came to Brazil knowing how to read and write, when the Portuguese, like early Americans, were the ignorant convicts, derelicts and marginals of their parental society.

    The Brazilian black did not get his nominal freedom until 1889; the last country to abolish slavery in this hemisphere was Brazil. Since then, the Brazilian black has been brainwashed by statements affirming that he is just as Brazilian as anyone else and that doors will be open as soon as he "cleanses his blood." The Brazilians who consciously glorify in their blackness are few. They are seen as eccentric. For example, Brother Abdias do Nascimento, black playwright and painter in exile here has lived somewhat of a lonely life. Most Brazilians, however, do celebrate Africanness, albeit unconsciously (such as dancing "samba" day in and out, eating African food as a natural part of life, and using words like dendê, bunda, macumba, saravá, capoeira, samba, etc.).

Much of the thrust of conscious Africanization in Brazil must come from the United States. American black people must start to realize that even some of the conceptualizations and solutions towards an *African* Africa will come from our efforts. The struggle is *one*.

It is shameful for Brazilian blacks in the southern states to be more exposed to German culture than to Africanness. In Blumenau[5] (dig the name), some blacks learn *German* before Portuguese!

It is shameful for a country with a least forty percent of its population black, to have less than one percent of that segment represented in the universities!

It is shame on Brazil to have to pass a law last year making it illegal to speak out on Brazilian racial discrimination and adjudicating one to three years as the corresponding sentence, plus one half of the original sentences added on if said statements are made before a group of people and/or get into the media![6]

It is a shame on American black people who do not make it their business to find out about and concern themselves with Africans throughout the world; who can travel to a country where experiences are so similar to ours that, as Brother Nascimento has said, the play, "In the Wine Time," could be called "In Cachaca Time"[7] and no other changes needed to depict urban Brazilian black life;—and yet who gratefully accept temporal admittance into Nescafe society at the expense of black people indigenous to that country!

And it is shame on me for not having taken the time to write these thoughts down sooner!

NOTES

1. Chairman of the Student Non-violent Coordinating Committee (SNCC) 1967–68.
2. A *pai-de-santo* or priest in Candomblé rites.
3. Thompson was an Afro-American journalist. The reference here is to a long feature essay she wrote about Brazil based on a trip there in 1965, "Does Amalgamation Work in Brazil?" *Ebony* 20 (July 1965), 27–41; and 20 (September 1965), 33–42. In a footnote Gilliam characterized Thompson's article as "a 'glowing' pro-assimilationist report."
4. In a recent note to her original essay Gilliam writes, "I am calculating 15 percent Amerindian. However, no one knows their number (pure Amerindians). These informal statistics are based upon the large urban centers where most of Brazil's population centers are located, the Amerindians being mostly in the northern rural section, and in the uncharted hinterlands."
5. A city founded by German immigrants in 1850 where German culture is still dominant.
6. The author is referring to the National Security Law of September 29, 1969, enacted by the military government to provide a legal basis for the punishment of anyone critical of its policies.
7. *Cachaca* is a popular, inexpensive Brazilian drink made from sugar cane.

22.

Leslie B. Rout, Jr., "Brazil: Study in Black, Brown and Beige"

> *Leslie B. Rout, Jr. (1936–87) was a professor of history at Michigan State University for twenty years. He wrote several books on Latin America, including* The African Experience in Spanish America *(1976). He traveled to Brazil several times as a jazz musician and scholar. He published three other articles on race relations in Brazil: "Sleight of Hand: Brazilian and American Authors Manipulate the Brazilian Racial Situation, 1910–1951,"* The Americas *24 (April 1973), 471–88; "Race Relations in Southern Brazil: The Pôrto Alegre Experience,"* Proceedings of the Pacific Coast Council on Latin American Studies *4 (1975), 89–100; and "Race and Slavery in Brazil,"* Wilson Quarterly *1 (August 1976), 73–89.*

IF YOU'RE like me, you've probably read Gilberto Freyre or Frank Tannenbaum, or watched a couple of CBS reports, paged through *Holiday* or some comparable journal. Perhaps you've talked to a Brazilian or two. If you've done any of these things, you know already that "no racial

From the *Negro Digest* 19 (February 1970), 21–23, 65–73. Reprinted by permission of Kathleen K. Rout.

problems exist in Brazil." Maybe the Brazilian you talked to was more discreet. He would then have informed you that there is less racial discrimination in Brazil than any place else in the world.

As the story is usually told, unlike the Anglo-Saxons who set up shop at Jamestown or Plymouth Rock, the Portuguese gentlemen who migrated to the new world had significantly fewer qualms about "nighttime integration." The result was that in addition to the obvious black slaves and white masters, there appeared an increasing myriad of colored persons who were part of both, but not really of either. Accordingly (and this is in keeping with the legend), the Brazilians adopted the converse of the formula adopted by the Anglo-Saxons. Where the English settled, any measure of Negro blood made you a Negro. In Brazil, any discernible quantity of white blood made you at least a *pardo* (mulatto). Ultimately, it was probably very much a question of what one could get those higher up in the pecking order to believe.

In today's United States of America, where racial troubles can no longer be swept under the carpet, the Brazilian legend exercises a peculiar influence. For Afro-Americans such as this writer, Brazil beckons as a kind of tropical Shangri-La. As a friend once put it, "Man, after I make my pile here, then I'm splitting for coffeeland where I can enjoy it." Others wonder how a nation which maintained slavery until May, 1888, where illiterates possibly outnumber literates, and where political democracy can hardly be said to have taken giant strides, could do what the "gringo Goliath" could not: satisfy the hopes and aspirations of its non-white citizens. . . .

In June, 1961, the Paul Winter Sextet, of which I was a member, won the Intercollegiate Jazz Festival held at Georgetown University. As fortune would have it, somebody in Washington, D.C., noticed that the six members of the group were split even-up—three blacks and three whites. Could you have dreamed of a better combination to send on a government-sponsored tour of Latin American colleges and universities? A seven-month tour was dropped into our laps. Secretly, I resolved that if Brazil resembled the land of Orpheus, José Carioca, Tannenbaum and Gilberto Freyre, it must eventually open its arms to a new immigrant—me.

Arriving in Pôrto Alegre (May, 1962), the first thing I tended to notice was that *brancos* in Brazil found nothing strange about fraternizing with Negroes. One saw *pretos* and *pardos* frequently, but as my Portuguese was limited to such terms as *macanudo* (and the usual unprintable terminology you always seem to learn first) it was nearly impossible to communicate with them. Exceedingly noticeable on the campuses of the university and in the theaters was the absence of Negroes at sextet concerts. Whites I questioned assured me that although the concerts were free, most Afro-Brazilians were of the lower economic classes, and rarely attended affairs where middle and upper class *Senhores* predominated. Previous experiences in South America had convinced me that some kind of class system would be found everywhere. The explanations given were logical, but in my opinion, insufficient. Somehow or another, I had to meet a few *pretos* and get their side of the story.

Jazz musicians meet their counterparts wherever they

seem to go in the world, and with the music as a medium, friendships are forged. Through Cepú, a black tenor saxophone player I met in a Rio nightclub, I finally met some *pretos* who spoke English. Speaking directly to the gentlemen (both of whom were musicians), I remarked that none of the black members of the sextet had encountered any incidences of discrimination in Brazil. One of the Brazilians smiled and said, "Things are not as they seem; they are more subtle here . . ." This was to be inkling number one, you might say.

In this regard, probably the most interesting character I would meet was a young Negro from Omaha, Nebraska, named Bill Waters. Waters had decided to take one year off, go to Brazil, and see whether he wanted to move there permanently. When I met him, his stay in Rio had exceeded ten months. He stated that while he liked Brazil, it had not been the racial nirvana he'd hoped to find. Indeed, he was amazed at the ease with which the black members of the sextet moved among Rio's social elite. He later confided in me that he felt certain that the prestige of the Department of State opened doors otherwise hermetically sealed. At the time, I was enjoying myself to such a degree that Waters' reservations seemed sour grapes. The whole issue reemerged about three months later when Bill stopped in Chicago on his way to Omaha. Having just returned to the U.S.A., I threw a small party and invited Waters. Afterwards he remarked, "You know Les, I saw more integration here tonight than I saw in twelve months in Brazil." What he really meant was miscegenation, and secretly I had to admit that while everywhere in Brazil one sees *pardos*, I had seen precious little intermingling on a social level. Admittedly, it was the *pretos* you saw pushing the brooms, but the witness of my own adventures as a musical diplomat in sambaland were a kind of insulation against the other reality. Bill was a great guy but. . . .

Two-and-one-half years would pass before I could again travel to Brazil. This time there would be no fanfare or ballyhoo. Under the guise of traveling graduate student doing dissertational research, one Les Rout would continue to investigate whether or not Brazil was where I wanted to belong. Fortunately my Portuguese had come along, and I had maintained contact with about half a dozen Brazilians I'd met the first time around. The years 1962–65 had convinced me that racial discrimination in the land of the free and home of the brave would end in 2965 at the earliest. Hopefully the Brazilians had more satisfactory answers. Boarding the jet, I could already hear João Gilberto singing *Samba da Minha Terra.*

There is the oft-told tale about the astronauts who landed on Mars, and were approached by one of its thirty-eyed, forty-legged, three-foot-high inhabitants. Despite their obvious disparity, the astronauts and the Martians got along fine. However, the latter cautioned the space travelers about one thing: "We don't want you messin' around with our females, you dig?"

There were times in Brazil when it occurred to me that I must have resembled an astronaut. For example, there was the time in late July, 1965, when I attended a theatre in Pôrto Alegre, in company with a fair young Brazilian girl of German parentage, whom I shall call Karen. There were, I believe, two shows that night. There was one on stage, and there was Karen and I. Probably everywhere except maybe New York and Paris, when black boys appear in polite society with attractive blondes, eyebrows go up a few inches and there is some gnashing of teeth. In Alabama, both of us would have been lynched. In Pôrto Alegre, they pointed their fingers, wagged their tongues and murdered us with their eyes. Never was I so happy to have the houselights dim and the play begin! At intermission, it started all over again however. The man sitting directly in front of me turned around so many times that I can still see in my mind where the moles were on his face. As for Karen, within five minutes she had been frightened out of her wits. After we joined a large group in a nightclub, she still could not relax. She agreed to dance with me only reluctantly, and then only after she had taken time to gauge the impact this even would have on the other customers. Violence? Naked force? There is nothing quite like social pressure to bully reluctant parties into line.

Later that night while reflecting on what had been a most unpleasant experience, I imagined myself calling Karen on the phone and hearing the maid answer—"She's not here. She just went out to visit all her remaining friends in Pôrto Alegre. She should be back in five minutes."

One might argue that despite its population of 800,000 Pôrto Alegre is hardly a center of cosmopolitanism. This is correct, but matters did not seem to be remarkably different in that haven of the hip, Rio de Janeiro. Still sharply in focus is the November evening on which I performed as special guest artist at the Boate K-Samba, for the Club de Jazz e Bossa Nova do Rio. Friends introduced me to a sparkling *branca* who taught Latin in a local private school. As is often the case when boy meets girl, boy asks girl if he might see her on another occasion. The young lady enthusiastically agreed to have dinner with me the following evening. Just before leaving the club with friends, the Afro-American again confirmed the date of the engagement with the Brazilian *branca*. Here is an approximation of the conversation that followed the next day:

He: "When may I come for you?"
She: "I am sorry, it is impossible."
He: "Well, how about lunch tomorrow?"
She: "That also is impossible."
He: "What about dinner tomorrow evening?"
She: "That is out of the question. I am sorry."
He: "Well, is it possible for me to visit you at all?"
She: "Unfortunately, there are problems . . . that also is impossible."

Checking with friends later, I discovered that the young lady was not married, had not come to the club with another man. I had not forced her to accept my invitation, or attempted to embarrass her. Assuming that I did not appear to be the previously described astronaut, did not have leprosy or trench mouth, the readers must pardon me if I chalked this experience up as another pigmentation misadventure.

Grounds for assuming the rationality of my initial speculation were provided about four days later. In the company of two acquaintances, I lay on the Copacabana beach, leering at the wild bikinis and encouraging my natural tan. The two associates were a white American called Ron (who was dodging the draft) and a luscious local product named Alicia. From time to time, Ron and Alicia would fall into heated clinches, oblivious to passersby. The beginning of the frantic sessions were cues for me to clamber to my feet and head for the salt water. It got pretty hectic after three trips, but not being a voyeur, I had no alternative other than head for home. Eventually Ron and Alicia reached some stage of fulfillment, and as the three of us sauntered along Avenida Atlântica, Ron asked me whether I wanted to accompany them to the movies that night. I had visions of a repeat of the afternoon's romantic interlude and this made a diplomatic response necessary: "Ron, like three is a crowd, man." Ron then asked Alicia whether she could produce a female companion for me that evening. Her reply was more than either of us had bargained for. "Senhores, there is much racial discrimination in the world." Enough said, sweetie. I never saw either one of them again.

Through a friend at the American Embassy, I met Ramon Andrade da Silvera, a *preto* lawyer. I wanted to ask him how he got along with young ladies who were not *pretas*, but we were not close friends; ask a question like that point-blank, and we might cease being acquaintances. As it developed, two nights before leaving Rio for New York, I got an answer without raising the question. Senhor da Silvera and I were drinking in one of the innumerable clubs that dot Avenida Atlântica. About three days before, da Silvera had phoned a young lady (a *branca* or *morena*, I forgot which), who was a friend of a friend of his. He had donned his most persuasive manner, and after hesitating, the young lady accepted an invitation to attend a party with him. At this point da Silvera informed the young lady that his skin more nearly approximated the color of chocolate ice cream than the vanilla variety. The young lady refused to believe him. For one thing, he spoke grammatically correct Portuguese, and the implication was that *pretos* (at least the ones she knew) were markedly deficient in this respect. He assured her, however, that he was at least one exception to the rule. Her reply closed the issue: "Well, if you are a *preto*, then I couldn't possibly go anywhere with you. My father would never permit it."

Senhor da Silvera was not particularly happy about the incident, and naturally I sympathized with him. Secretly though, I felt some relief. Apparently there were other astronauts loose in Brazil! How wonderful it was to know that one did not have a concealed case of leprosy or trench mouth. Now perhaps if da Silvera and I had been *pardos*.

Some of the incidents during my 1965 sojourn in the land of coffee, Ipanema and the Amazon River were humorous, some were exasperating, but there was at least one that I never did figure out. One drizzly night in São Paulo, I decided before heading for a friend's apartment, that I'd better have a shave. In mid-town São Paulo, finding a barbershop is not exactly the easiest task in the world. I approached two well-dressed *pretos*, and asked them the directions to the nearest barbershop. They were quite helpful, and within ten minutes, I found the place I believed they'd directed me to. I walked in. The first barber who saw me did a double take, dropped his straight razor and stood there gaping. The rest of the clientele looked at me as if somehow or another, I had crossed the Rubicon with ten divisions, or maybe wiped out two platoons of Viet Cong singlehandedly.

Since I was already in the door, there was nothing to do except brazen it out. Ignoring the stares of about half-a-dozen customers and four barbers, I took a chair and buried my head in a handy copy of O *Cruzeiro*. Finally it was my turn. You guessed it; I got the barber who'd earlier dropped his razor in shock. Visions of a slit throat flitted through my mind. I muttered that a quick shave would be my pleasure, and sincerely hoped it wouldn't be my last.

Not one word was exchanged until half way down one cheek, the barber asked, "Senhor, what country are you from?" He just knew that I couldn't be a Brazilian. After I explained to him that I was an American, from "the city of Al Capone and his friends," the service became more courteous. After leaving the shop, I made a fast tour of the area looking for another barbershop. I didn't find one. It became obvious that *pretos* (and possibly *pardos* too) just didn't seek service in that establishment. My entrance suggested that I was either a foreigner or a social revolutionary. But why had the two *pretos* sent me to a place they seemingly did not patronize? Did they think I'd be tossed out on my ear?

Perhaps the most exasperating occurrence of them all took place on a São Paulo street one mid-afternoon. A policeman tried to have me jailed for vagrancy (i.e., my pants were accidentally unzipped, and I was unshaven). Fortunately, another officer came to the conclusion that the gentleman in the passport photo and the unshaven character who was trying to establish his innocence were one and the same. Finally, I was allowed to zip up my pants and move on. Thank the Lord that a Brazilian jail was not to be my destination, but I had to ask myself whether or not the policeman would have stopped me if I had been white.

Almost as trying was the problem of entering apartment buildings in São Paulo and Rio. The call-up system which prevails in hi-rise apartments in Chicago, New York, etc., is not the vogue in the posh districts of Brazilian cities. Instead, there is usually a doorman of sorts, and after he goes home (perhaps 10:00 or 11:00 P.M.), street level entrances are usually locked. Thus, if you don't have a key, the party you're visiting had better be downstairs awaiting your arrival.

At least six times, I have entered apartment buildings to visit friends (in each case, *brancos*), only to be stopped by the doorman, who then conducted a minor court of inquisition in the hallway before allowing me to proceed. I say at least six times, because on these occasions I followed a *branco* into the building. In each case, the white person was not stopped, but I was. Conceivably, the other party lived in the building, or was known to the doorman, but then again perhaps he was not. In any case, I mentioned the incidents chiefly because the white person who entered the building ahead of me did not greet the doorman or receive a greeting. It should be also noted that whenever I entered an apartment building via the servants' entrance, no one ever asked me any questions. Perhaps my housemaid's knee was a little too obvious.

Even more intriguing were the situations I encountered in the Copacabana apartment building in which I lived for a week with David Kurick, ex–Tufts University Professor, and in 1965, a USIA trainee. Using my key to enter the building late at night, on at least one occasion I found myself confronted by residents who blocked the stairs and demanded to know what I was doing in the building. Situations like this can be very tense, but I soon discovered a procedure that alleviated such problems. Yanking out my passport and shouting "Americano, Americano," was the equivalent of Ali Baba's "Open Sesame." The fear on the part of the apartment house dwellers that burglars might penetrate the locked street entrance was justifiable, but apparently a black man with an American passport wouldn't do such a thing. Some *preto* without such a document was a logical suspect.

And then there was the funny old landlady who had the penthouse next to Kurick's. When Dave told her that a "Negro friend of his" would be moving in for a short time, she just had to visit and discover what kind of man this was. I don't believe she really thought I had two heads; maybe it was more a case of what kind of "Negro friend" was this that Kurick was willing to share his apartment with? Eventually, she and I became more or less chummy. One afternoon over coffee, she told me that she had been astounded in New York (she had been there twice) by the tremendous number of large, shiny automobiles the Negro population seemed to possess. Initially, she believed most of the Negroes to be chauffeurs, but gradually she concluded that many of the autos belonged to the people who were driving them. "When I returned to Rio and told my friends about this," she said, "they refused to believe me." In a sense, I can understand her mystification. For what it's worth, I never met a *preto* in Brazil who owned an automobile, and never rode in a taxicab driven by one.

It was a Sunday night in Pôrto Alegre, and I had been invited to the home of Erico Veríssimo, the internationally known novelist. There were a large number of relatives and friends in the living room, women and children on one side, while each male drank various liquors and attempted to insure that in the verbal exchanges, he didn't get caught with his punch line down. The freewheeling conversation turned to racial prejudice in the United States. As rapidly as possible, I turned the issue slightly by reciting a few of my more "interesting" experiences in Brazil. Senhor Veríssimo politely inquired whether my imagination had perhaps run rampant. I assured him that a Negro born in the United States either developed his own personal radar system, or became psychotic trying to differentiate racial slurs from accidental incidents; I did not yet believe myself to be psychotic. Other participants in this discussion were two male relatives of Senhor Veríssimo. When I had finished speaking, one of them smiled and said, "Didn't you know? There's all kinds of racial discrimination in Brazil." The other gentleman became red in the face and blurted out, "There is no racial discrimination in Brazil!" The two of them argued the question hotly for perhaps twenty minutes. Meanwhile I kept my mouth shut. Here were two *brancos* heatedly discussing the alleged possibility of racial discrimination in Brazil, but who had discriminated against them? Of course if they had desired my opinion, they would doubtless have asked for it. They didn't.

Reflections

Although these events took place about four years ago, it was literally impossible for me to write them until now. Quite foolishly, I had assumed that there was a Land of Oz, that there really was a "somewhere over the rainbow." My journey to Brazil had put me eyeball to eyeball with grim reality. Black boy, you can run, but you cannot hide!

Some may conclude from what I have written that neither *pretos* or most *pardos* can aspire to greatness in Brazil. This is hardly the case. Among the more celebrated *pretos* and/or *pardos* (and here, I include everyone whom I would conceive as being considered a Negro if they were in this country), are Pelé (Edson Arantes), the soccer star who grosses $200,000 a year, such personal friends as Jair

Rodrigues and Lenni Andrade, vocalists, Raul de Santos ("Raulzinho"), musician, and Antentor Carlos Vaz, artist. It is not my intention to denounce all whites as being deluded or racists. People are people all over the world. Gradually, the hate and disillusionment subsided. Eventually it became possible to make some kind of reasonably objective comparisons:

FIRST. In the United States of America, the installation of the Jim Crow system forced mulattoes and blacks together. Mulattoes did not prefer things that way, but they were unable to force any significant change in the situation. Thus, while "light" Negroes and darker ones remained at odds for many years, the inability of parleying lightness into privilege brought about a black unity that would not have been possible in 1900. If you question this supposition, take a good look at Adam Clayton Powell. Considering that God supposedly draws good from every evil act, one might say that "Whitey" did us a favor.

In Brazil, the official ideology is "Brazilianization," or more accurately, amalgamation of the races. The general impetus, however, is toward "whitening" the nation. The *pardos*, therefore, distinguish themselves from the *pretos*, for they see themselves as farther along the lightening process than their "brothers." A *preto* might consider himself as marrying "up," if he could forge an alliance with a *pardo*, but a lighter-skinned female would be considered as marrying "down." Indeed, animosity between *pardos* and *pretos* seemed very strong in Brazil. One might well ask if some kind of race war occurred in Brazil, which way would the *pardos* go? It has also passed through my mind that possibly the cleverest way to keep non-whites divided would be to perpetrate a system whereby *pardos* yearn to become lighter, and *pretos* yearn to become *pardos*.

SECOND. From an economic standpoint, the Afro-American appears much more prosperous in general than *pretos* or *pardos* in Brazil. This is a simple reflection of the fact that the United States of America is a richer nation than the United States of Brazil. In neither nation can it be argued that non-whites had an equitable share of whatever there was to get. However, migration to the northern urban areas and three major wars since 1917–18 have put Afro-Americans in a position where some of the funds that came their way could be invested or used to buy property.

Most amazing to this observer was the almost total absence of Afro-Brazilians in the business world. In the industrial south of Brazil, where miscegenation is hardly a virtue, one hardly expected to see *preto* bank executives. But even in the northern areas, *preto* or dark *pardo* bank or office clerks were as rare as de Gaulle supporters in the State Department. Apparently, the *brancos* owned everything. *Pretos* and *pardos* might sing, dance and play soccer, but the mysteries of commerce were somehow beyond their grasp.

During the past five years, the events of my Brazilian adventures have continued to influence my outlook on many problems, often times providing insights which otherwise would have been unavailable. For example, in the last five years, there has been much talk in some Afro-American circles about the "third world," and the possible collaboration of all oppressed peoples in destroying western imperialism and "liberating" non-whites from white oppressors. It is here that my journeys to Brazil had perhaps their greatest influence: Witness the disillusionment of some Black Panthers as a result of their treatment in

Castro's Cuba, the bloody struggle between blacks and Arabs in the Sudan, the continuing bitterness between blacks and East Indians in Guyana, or the black revolt against Indonesians in West Irian. The assumption underlying the "third world" concept is the belief that once western imperialism goes the way of the dodo, all will be love, strawberries and doin' your thing. But I came to know Brazilian Marxists who ranted about U.S. imperialism but clammed up when I wanted to talk about racial barriers in Rio or São Paulo. Ever so well, I remember the mulattoes who saw no relationship either between themselves and darker-skinned parties in Brazil or the U.S.A. Most of all, I cannot forget the fact that most black Brazilians were curious about their North American brothers, but had no intention of aiding Mississippi sharecroppers in their struggle. In brief, the "third world" idea suggests that the departure of the white oppressor practically assures the future cooperation of non-white peoples. Yeah, sure it does.

Soul brother, take heed: There is no Land of Oz! Whatever advances our people make, we will most likely have to make them by ourselves.

23.

Cleveland Donald, Jr., "Equality in Brazil: Confronting Reality"

> *Cleveland Donald, Jr., is a university administrator and Latin American historian whose specialty is Brazil. His 1973 dissertation at Cornell University was titled "Slavery and Abolition in Campos, Brazil, 1830–1888." Donald has taught at the University of Mississippi (where he earned his B.A. in 1966), the State University of New York at Binghamton, and the University of Massachusetts at Amherst. He is currently director of the University of Connecticut campus at Waterbury.*

THE UNITED STATES of Brazil has been exempted from the scathing and critical scrutiny that other countries, at a similar state of development, generally experience. To be sure, scholarly and popular use of such terms as "underdeveloped," "backward," or even the more positive "developing," often betrays a disdain for and condescension toward the area. Yet, even with persistent rumors of the extermination of the Indian population, urban guerilla

From *Black World* 22 (November 1972), 23–34. Reprinted by permission of the author.

warfare, and other salient social problems, Brazil receives more than its share of favorable treatment, being tagged as one of the few stable Latin American democracies, a non-violent state, and a good ally.

This praise of Brazil is nowhere more manifest than in North American attitudes toward Brazilian race relations and race policy. In the United States, during most discussions of the problem of race, Brazil is invariably cited as an example of interracial harmony and the paradigm of racial assimilation. This tendency among the general public to hold Brazil as a model of the ideal interracial society is by no means recent. The belief has its origins far back in Brazilian history when Brazilian slaveholders, through domination of the society, implanted in the national consciousness the concept of the legitimate and benign character of the slave system and the principles of race relations it expressed. The propagation of the image acquired external support from North American abolitionists and reformers who contrasted its gentle character with the harsh and cruel aspects of the southern United States variety.

But the prevalence of the favorable image of Brazilian race relations, here and there, becomes more problematic when, pursuing the historical records, one finds that parallel to and often contrasted with this mild view there exists another attitude. Within the records left by foreign travelers and Brazilian reformers and, more important, from the testimony of Blacks themselves—written in the form of slave revolts then and fraternal work songs and jokes today—one discovers the Brazilian experience to be one long tale of cruelty, racial atrocities, and continual warfare. . . . Yet, the benign image remains. One asks: How and why has it survived to the virtual exclusion of the other more critical view? An answer to such an inquiry elicits a description and reappraisal of contemporary racial attitudes and behavior currently operative there, and in the symbiotic relationship between the Brazilian and the United States' racial patterns.

II

Part of the reason for the popularity in both countries of the view of benign Brazilian race relations resides in North Americans' attitudes towards their own race problem. Here, both Blacks and whites, for different reasons, tend to accept the approved notion of Brazil. Most Blacks have had their image of Brazilian race relations fashioned by popular Black-oriented periodicals, like *Ebony*, which generally concentrate upon, portray, and mystify the exceptional cases—implicitly perhaps seeking to preserve, through such a procedure, Black pride and to inspire racial uplift. The presentation of the Black experience through the medium of the hero, rather than the exaltation of the common people, was necessitated by the nature of the historical materials available, the limits placed on the uses of such materials by a white-policed Black-intellectual ideology, and the intellectual shortcomings of Black scholarship (this last due to the first two). The Brazilian experiment, by virtue of its geographical remoteness, its racial composition, and its myth of interracial well-being, was very much worth watching.

North American Black readers' attitudes toward the idealized versions of Brazilian race relations are determined primarily by their psychological relationship to whites and white society. Many Blacks either enjoy or aspire to enjoy a rightful share of mobility and social goods. They entertain the vision of self- and social improvement, and generally view "boring from within" or change inside the society—whether for reformist or revolutionary reasons—as the most practicable procedure at this juncture in the Black experience. At best, marginally located in the social system and constantly confronted with acts of hostility by white Americans, ranging from the most conservative to the most liberal, Blacks see in Brazil a society where Black and white live harmoniously and where Blacks can find peace and an integral place within a white-dominated national structure. The immediate consequence of this attitude is the removal of race as an immutable or as a constant factor in the resolution of United States' domestic social problems. The idealized Brazilian case proves that some whites are capable of humanity toward Blacks and, consequently, implies that certain technical and cultural changes in the United States might result in a social system akin to her neighbor's to the south. In this sense, the myth of the Brazilian social situation might be seen as a device for social control. Indeed, the device works on Brazilian Blacks as well, for Afro-Brazilians who believe (or internalize) white myths of social harmony not only tolerate their own oppressive system but feel sorry for Black Americans as well.

The Brazilian model of interracial adjustment serves a wide spectrum of needs in the North American white community. Conservatives might find the idea tolerable because of its suppressive effects on Blacks. At the same time, what was said of the Utopian vision held by Blacks is doubly true for American liberals, who carry with them a heritage replete with Utopian fantasies. Cast off by the old European societies, the ancestors of American liberals came to this country to create a perfect social order. However, failing to do no more than establish the ordinary imperfect society, they reinvigorated liberalism in order to improve upon the initial effort. Whenever in the analysis of domestic racial problems the question of a suitable model arises, Brazil, resplendent in all the exoticism, primitivism, and eroticism associated with its tropical climate and developing status, is offered by liberals as the exemplary community. Inebriated by Brazilian propaganda about its situation, the North American liberal comes to view that country's racial behavior more as a consequence of cautious social planning rather than social backwardness....

III

In the past, the idealized image of Brazilian racial behavior took on diplomatic significance when it was used by Brazilians to assert equality with, and, on rare occasions, superiority over North American social life. Brazilians admitted that the United States easily excelled in technological know how and industrial advancement. But this concession was quickly followed by a deprecation of American racial policy and an assertion of the superiority of their own racial situation. Thus, the presumption of Brazilian racial advancement functioned as the equalizer which allowed the trade-off of technical excellence for social superiority. The readiness to exchange implied that its proponents were friendlily disposed toward the American way of life and Brazilian–American relations.

Often, Brazilians suggested that their racial policy entitled them to claim general superiority over North Americans. Believing that the primary motive for technological development was, or ought to have been, human social progress, they argued that improvement of society was qualitatively far more significant than perfection of technology. These chauvinists concluded that they generally were better than North Americans since their nation predominated, by virtue of a sage race policy, in that aspect of nationhood that was qualitatively more important. Camouflaging the subtle articulation of anti-Americanism, this view's adherents were sharply critical of and often opposed to the United States system, particularly in those areas that touch upon Brazilian–American relations.

The astute Black visitor to Brazil soon realizes that the constant and vigorous protestations against the presence of prejudice and discrimination in Brazil can be the most powerful testament to their existence. If Brazilians have no racial problems, why do they devote an inordinate amount of energy to affirming racial harmony? Whenever a Black American meets a white Brazilian, the conversation invariably begins with consideration by the Brazilian of the race issue, a statement that he, personally, harbors no prejudice against Blacks and an inquiry from him about whether the Black visitor has witnessed or experienced racism during his stay in the country. The inquiry into the Black American's Brazilian experiences, particularly the dubious way in which it is approached, implicitly acknowledges the possibility of racial bias. . . .

The white Brazilian generally places undue stress on the symbolic demonstrations of a lack of prejudice. If a Black Brazilian is on hand—even (or particularly) if he or she is a servant—the white will bestow embraces and fraternal kisses as signs of affection. Although done to buttress his argument, Brazilian stratification and informal social distance render such gestures meaningless except as expressions of social etiquette, or of paternalism and condescension. Indeed, the social connotations of these acts, given the norms of the society, make it possible for the white to feign equality without threatening the already existing relationship between the Black and himself. Furthermore, when interpreted in this sense as a projection of his desired relationship with the Black visitor, the white Brazilian's perception of his relationship with the Black Brazilian means that he does not intend to accept the Black outsider as an equal or to allow him the mobility he might have enjoyed in another society.

Beyond making a pretension to racial equality feasible without violating the unstated assumptions underlying Brazilian Black–white relations, the external gestures mentioned earlier are also required in order to preserve and to perfect these norms of behavior and to weave the Brazilian social fabric. In order to control the community, the *élite* must profess such beliefs themselves and require the masses to do the same. Brazilians always cling to such outward manifestations: Black and white attend the same school; there is interracial marriage; there are no separate ghettoes or communities for Blacks; and there are no Jim Crow laws. They argue that the letter of the law and the expressed attitudes are pro-integration, sympathetic to Blacks, and without bias. However, the observer finds that racial violence is submerged and clandestine and parallels other types of hidden hostility pervading much of Brazilian life. The number of educated Blacks is infinitesimal, the number of interracial marriages outside poverty-ridden communities is equally small, and the number of community-less Blacks is staggering.

The maintenance of Brazilian race relations at or near the *status quo* necessitates—in addition to the symbolic homage to racial brotherhood—the continuous use of covert violence, sometimes physical, but always psychological. Overt manifestations of racial animosity, however, threaten the stated norms under which the society operates, and, consequently, rebels are subtly silenced or ostracized. Perfect examples of the manner in which the society deals with potential troublemakers exist historically in the numerous instances of the slavemaster's violent response to any slave attempt to establish and perpetuate a visible separate community. Today, they are seen whenever Brazilians proclaim the presence of African influences in the culture, and, at the same time, attach a plethora of negative values and connotations to them.

The Black North American's immediate reaction to the social situation upon arrival in Brazil determines whether and to what extent he will personally share in the overt coercion heaped upon the Black Brazilian rebel or in the covert coercion suffered by the average Afro-Brazilian. In fact, his answer to the question whether he has witnessed or experienced racism in Brazil is solicited, not to encourage an honest assessment of actual racial practices, but to determine the kind of treatment to be accorded him. For most Brazilians, an affirmation of Brazilian racism amounts to a straightforward criticism of, and attack upon, expressed racial values; while a negative or qualified conclusion implies their acceptance. Those who respond, yes, will be met by overt violence, ostracism, and forms of hostile discrimination; but those who reply, no, will be tolerated and gradually disciplined into "their place." As regards the Afro-American's behavior, if he wears a bush (a sign of rebelliousness, African-ness, primitiveness), he will be feared, harassed, and intimidated until he has it cut, leaves town, or proves that having it does not suggest rebelliousness. Thereafter, he will receive only the normal treatment of Brazilian racism. He may be cleanly dressed in order to be a credit to his race (and Brazilian racial policy), but must not dress too well, for this could well be seen as an indication of his over-aggressiveness.

The Brazilian race rationale—designed to maintain the nation's interracial image, contradicted by the ferocity of its propagation, and strengthened by gestures and unseen violence rather than open animosity—is not really believed by most Brazilians. The white recognizes the contradiction between citing interracial marriage as an example of Brazilian racial equality and commenting that every Black wishes to marry a white because he feels inferior and desires self-improvement. That Blacks might choose whites suggests that the society is biased toward whites. Moreover, since many whites often offer these contradictions with a mischievous glint in both eyes, it appears that such inconsistencies are intentional. In the underdeveloped world in which he lives, the white Brazilian cannot possibly make contrasts between haves and havenots, in terms of nations, without ending up on the short end of the ledger. But contrasts between him and the Afro-Brazilians are possible, and made all the more necessary because, in the international hierarchy of development, there is little else that he can look down on. Thus, while they do not wish their racism articulated verbally and openly, white Brazilians take great pains in having it informally and unconsciously understood that theirs is a white country. Blacks, in particular, are subtly taught this because their behavior and attitude can prove the contrary or bring the contradictions into the open. The respect Blacks give to the assumption of white superiority forms part of a circle that is closed when whites subsequently point to Black behavior to justify the reality and maintain the ideal. The situation is an uneasy one where whites, unsure of themselves, depend on Black quiescence to preserve and validate the rationale by which they function.

Ironically, one way to fathom how Brazilians see themselves is through a description and analysis of their conceptualization of the American race problem. A Black American visiting Brazil and speaking fluent Portuguese with only a trace of an accent might be asked if he is from Bahia (or Africa, as second choice). If the Black states that he is a United States citizen, the white Brazilian generally would respond, first, that he had not known that America had Blacks, and then contradict himself by adding that he had heard the United States was a good country with a horrible race problem. After some thought, the bewildered Black might eventually surmise that the Brazilian knows that there are Blacks in the United States; but, given the Brazilian's knowledge of racial discrimination in the United States and the Brazilian's own racial bias, no Black would be in a position to afford the long voyage south.

Using the North American racial pattern as the model, or at the least as another justification for an already established pattern, the white Brazilian is not ashamed of his real behavior and attitude towards Blacks. Discrimination and prejudice are treated as components of the "civilizing" process, particularly when discovered as recent or increasing phenomena associated with urbanization, industrialization, and the breakdown of paternalism and traditionalism. Racial bigotry is regarded as an unpleasant but unavoidable consequence of the national effort to take its place among the developed and civilized nations of the world. In the white Brazilian's eyes, the United States has thrived on, allegedly, the most brutal forms of capitalistic slavery and segregation. Neither American companies located in Brazil nor the American embassy has any Blacks in key positions. All arguments point the Luso-Brazilian toward one conclusion: Brazil joins an honorable club when it abuses its Black citizens.

The major participants in the formation of the contemporary Brazilian racial pattern are, or course, the Afro-Brazilians. The degree to which the Black Brazilian has or has not constructed successful defenses against the total emasculation of his personality remains one of the most bitterly discussed issues of Brazilian Black–white relations, and the key to an accurate prognostication of the future of the myths and the realities of the Brazilian racial dilemma. However, since their ability to survive has depended to a significant degree on their behavior and their apparent acquiescence to the public image of themselves, it is extremely difficult to gauge the extent to which Black Brazilians have believed the dominant descriptions and stereotypes of their personality. Nor is it easy to determine the extent to which they might use such stereotypes and attitudes to prevent more profound intrusions upon their way of life. It is difficult to know in depth how they view their world.

A few comments can be made about the Afro-Brazilians' perceptions of the Brazilian racial problem, however. The Black Brazilian knows that in order to sustain the belief that Brazil is a true interracial society, it has been necessary for white Brazilians to prevent the overt existence of a separate, integral Brazilian Black community of the type which thrives here under *de jure* and *de facto* segregation. He finds, according to the myths enveloping Brazilian race relations, that he has been assimilated under a number of conditions, usually when he has light skin, straight hair, an extensive formal education, or a spouse of the white race. However, because the African aspects of his personality are de-emphasized and eventually eradicated, this process of assimilation actually strips him of his identifiable racial characteristics, that is, his physical features, and his cultural heritage. Consequently, the Afro-Brazilian knows that Brazilian assimilation has never accepted the African—only a white man in a Black skin.

On the other hand, the reality, in contrast to the myth, has taught the Afro-Brazilian that a Black skin could never cover a white man. He has realized what is under our segregated system an *a priori* assumption: under no circumstance can he be tolerated as an equal. If some Blacks can enjoy upward mobility, some whites might be displaced and experience downward mobility; furthermore, if Blacks are allowed the potential for equality, Brazilian whites would no longer have the absolute measure by which they could distinguish themselves from the world's unfortunates. The Afro-Brazilians know innately that the racial adjustments said to be occurring in Brazil do not involve the question of their equality, but of their continued relegation to an inferior status. While the forms of prejudice and discrimination vary historically, the old attitudinal and behavioral patterns established between master and slave, superior and inferior, nonetheless have remained the same. Ultimately, the Afro-Brazilians' dilemma is a peculiar one: they must believe that they can attain an equality that is unattainable by that behavior required of them.

If one is fortunate enough to establish rapport with a Black Brazilian, one can appreciate the challenges posed by the unique aspects of his experience. At first contact, the Afro-Brazilian might automatically comment that "we do not have racism here." Told that Brazil does have a serious race problem, he might initially respond that your observations are distortions brought on by your having been a victim of a horrible North American experience. Eventually, the Black Brazilian finally might agree with his own question—one that explains his earlier reluctance—"Yes, but what can I do about it?" Myth in this case appears to be less exacting than reality.

IV

The Afro-Brazilian, observing the rise of Black militancy in the United States and the absence of it in Brazil, will not find an explanation in the existence in Brazil of a Black community divided by the national acceptance of a color spectrum that is manifold with infinite gradations between the extremes of black and white. The color spectrum is by no means unique to Brazil; it flourishes wherever Blacks and whites come into contact. Moreover, the Brazilian color spectrum produces a strange and unexpected result: while one can condemn the fact of only one category for Blacks in the United States as a technique for the dehumanization of Afro-Americans, in Brazil the presence of infinite variations in color results in the same type of Black dehumanization. During slavery, and to a limited extent even today, the Afro-Brazilian can be born a mulatto, reared a *preto*, live the life of a *pardo*, and be buried a *moreno*. But this does not mean that white Brazilians regard Blacks as human beings any more than white Americans do; for the power of self-definition in the Brazilian case lies beyond the control of Afro-Brazilians, in the hands of whites. The fact that white Brazilians can define Blacks as they please contributes to the anxiety and frustration that makes possible the easy co-optation and psychological emasculation of Blacks. In this sense, color gradations in the context of the Brazilian cultural *milieu* are a disadvantage rather than an advantage.

Nor do clues to understanding the Brazilian and North American racial experiences lie in the concept of the mulatto. If we accept the view of a mulatto society as desirable, the racial situation in Brazil no longer becomes one of Black versus white, and one would expect an absence of anti-mulatto racial bigotry there expressed in a positive treatment of and attitude toward mulattoes. But if the average mulatto's experiences are different in degree and kind from that of the average Afro-Brazilian, then how does one account for a radical mulatto abolitionist like José do Patrocinio, or for mulattoes who have attempted with other Blacks to form Afro-Brazilian civil rights organizations, and for those today who continue to express in a large body of literature an awareness of the prejudice and discrimination common to other Blacks? Moreover, the mulatto and a varied color spectrum occur in the United States as well as in Brazil; white Brazilians exploit color distinctions directly by expressly encouraging and rewarding them, while white North Americans do so indirectly by clandestinely encouraging and rewarding them. Furthermore, it is important not to attach significance to the contention that in Brazil the mulatto is not a "Negro" while in the United States (due to an emphasis of genotype) he is. For one reason, being "Negro" in Brazil is far more pejorative, dangerous, and unsettling than in the United States. Hence, the Afro-American visiting Brazil does not ponder over the causes of Black militancy in the United States and its absence in Brazil, but over the meaning of Black militancy within the North American cultural context. Those labeled "Negroes" in Brazil find all doors to advancement closed to them, but in the United States,

"Negroes" have often found the doors of opportunity ajar, and some psychological contentment, whenever they affirmed their "Negroness." In fact, it does not matter that the Brazilian mulatto is not "Negro"; far more important is the fact that he is never white. Whenever mulattoes are regarded as white in Brazil, they are invariably "passing," a phenomenon very much a part of the United States racial scene. The mulatto personifies the interloper in a racially polarized world: whites tolerate the mulatto, and are comforted by his presence, because mulattoes do not confront them somatically, or as a phenotype, with the threat of the African presence; at the same time, whites abuse the mulatto because, since he only closely resembles them, they can still distinguish him from themselves and use those distinctions as a measure by which they can positively judge themselves. The mulatto is different, not so different as to trouble the Brazilian mind, but just different enough to be used as a negative model of self-appraisal. Under such circumstances, the mulattoes' experiences are generally as bad as those of darker Afro-Brazilians.

Even though the biological manner of his creation is frowned upon, the mulatto represents the ideal "Negro" in the United States and Brazil because whites see him as an emasculated African. Considered not as a solution but as escape from a racial situation (like the Brazilian emphasis on phenotypes and somatic norms and the United States' stress on genotype and psychic norms), the mulatto concept serves only remotely as a clue to the similarities and differences in the Brazilian and North American racial experiences. One need not contrast attitudes towards biology and physical appearances, or look for escape hatches. The general anti-African bias in Brazil and the United States constitutes the key to an understanding of the two nations' racial experiences. This bias implies that the issue is beyond Black, white, and mulatto somewhere in the tensions created from the clash of two cultures. Hence, the study of the two basically hostile cultures, one profoundly African and the other European.

Prejudice and discrimination against all people of color exists in the same intensity in both Brazil and the United States. At first glance, Brazilian prejudice and discrimination have distinctive manifestations, thus accounting for the superficial similarities and differences in the Brazilian and North American experiences; but the Afro-American observer knows that those forms vary dramatically in Brazil, itself, and that they transcend national boundaries, for each expression has appeared, and often predominated, in the United States at some place, at some time, and most importantly in some particular situation of interaction between African and European cultures. . . . The Afro-American leaves Brazil sensing that the ultimate explanation and solution to the racial situations in both countries lie in the utilization of a Pan-African intellectual approach.

V

The idealized Brazilian racial situation has been Brazil's greatest source of shame and pride. Unstripped of racial paternalism, the apparent Brazilian racial reality was—and to some extent still is—that nation's redeeming grace. On its strength, the country is as well off as, if not better than, the United States. Yet, times are changing so that the influence of racial paternalism decreases (at least among the liberal intellectuals and the poor) as racial conflict increases in a more open, competitive society.

Flux has created a confusing pattern and one pauses to reflect that old Brazilian attitudes toward its racial policies will more and more give way to new attitudes reflecting clashes between the races. Class and cultural differences, long held as explanations of why Luso-Brazilians have and Afro-Brazilians have not, will become recognized as subtle forms of discrimination and segregation. For those who sincerely believe in the old viewpoint, and particularly for those Black and white Brazilians who have benefitted from it, the change will be traumatic; they may lash out in anger and from frustration at the exponents of the new order. They may see this change as a detriment to Brazilian Black–white relations and as a sure-fire way of bringing on racial holocaust and terminating the reputed process of gradual assimilation which occurred under the old order.

Those who accept such change, as well as those who stand to benefit from it, will emphasize the good of it all. For them, conflict and protest will be more rewarding than nonviolence and conversation. Blacks and sympathetic whites will form groups like the NAACP or provide support for leaders like Booker T. Washington. Perhaps, a man of Marcus Garvey's stature and bent will appear on the scene. The Black community will progress materially as much as it has in the United States.

On the other hand, looking at the United States, one might conclude that, given the thrust of "integration," urban renewal, and other forces disintegrating the Black community, Black and white Americans' attitudes and actions will shift gradually toward the traditional views held by Brazilians. The shift might not be difficult since the traditional South's attitudes have always resembled the old Brazilian attitudes. The notion of Black contentment, the tendency to stress economic factors—these beliefs and others will become important under an integration characterized by the negative assumptions of inferior Black lifestyle and behavior. Integration will make views that have been historically sectional, or allegedly Brazilian, become national in scope.

Then again, one might find that in Brazil and in the United States there have been other historical instances similar to the processes now at work in both countries. The numerous occasions when racial paternalism has been advocated in the United States by Blacks and whites need not be recited. In Brazil, the old Afro-Brazilian abolitionist, José do Patrocinio, described by one of his Brazilian biographers as the "tiger of abolition," could well be called, if he were alive today, the Black Panther of abolition. The material variations shaping the racial situation in both countries may explain attitudinal changes from period to period; but, the basic spiritual state of the Brazilian and American racial dilemma has not changed. For, as the debate continues over which has been freer, the Afro-American slave or the Afro-Brazilian slave, one can never forget that both are nonetheless slaves.

24.

Richard L. Jackson, " 'Mestizaje' vs. Black Identity: The Color Crisis in Latin America"

> Richard L. Jackson is perhaps the leading North American student of Afro–Spanish American literature and of the treatment of blacks in Latin American literature. Among his books are The Black Image in Latin American Literature *(1976)*, Black Writers in Latin America *(1979), and* Black Literature and Humanism in Latin America *(1988). He is a graduate of Knoxville College, Tennessee, and Ohio State University. He has taught Spanish at Carleton University in Ottawa, Canada, since 1963.*

IN DISCUSSING the development of Afro–Latin American cultural patterns from the early days of the Spanish Colonial Empire to the Afro-Cuban Movement in this century, Martha K. Cobb recently emphasized in *Black World* that research on the Spanish-speaking Americas would add another dimension to Black people's awareness of ourselves and our common identity by confirming what has long been suspected—namely, that there is a pattern in the African contact with Western civilization that, despite differences of language and life-style, can be traced wherever

From *Black World* 24 (July 1975), 4–21. Reprinted by permission of the author.

Black men and women have been situated.* This pattern, characterized largely by white racism, slavery and racial oppression, has had a great impact on the ethnic survival of Black people in Latin America, where another pattern, equally traceable, has emerged on a wide scale to threaten their ethnic and cultural identity. This second pattern is embodied in the concept of miscegenation or *mestizaje*, a process that, while loosely defined as ethnic and cultural fusion, is often understood to mean the physical, spiritual and cultural rape of Black people.

For, despite artistic expressions of Black themes, Blacks in Latin America have had to wage a constant battle against extinction through cultural fusion or acculturation and particularly through racial amalgamation. The strong process of miscegenation running throughout the history of Latin America would seem to refute the existence of a pattern of racial conflict in that part of the world. The two phenomena, however, are not mutually exclusive, especially if there is any truth in the assertion, put in its bluntest form, that whites try to get rid of Blacks in the United States through extermination (and birth control) and in Latin America through racial amalgamation, or *linchamiento étnico* or *branco* ("ethnic" or "white lynching"), as the process has been called. Just as cultural fusion, and in some instances government pressures, have not encouraged the development and existence of a separate Black cultural heritage, the process of racial bleaching denies the Latin American Black the recognizable African characteristics of his physical features and thus his Black identity.

Black people existed in some areas of Latin America

---

*Martha K. Cobb, "Africa in Latin America: Customs, Culture, Literature," *Black World* 21, no. 10 (August 1972), 6.

and even predominated in others where today they are hardly visible. Although statistics vary, Blacks outnumbered whites, for example, in Lima, Peru, in the latter half of the sixteenth century. And until the mid-eighteenth century the ratio of slaves to Spaniards in Mexico City was two or three to one. In 1810, more than half the population of Venezuela was made up of Blacks. And Black people were important elements in the population of Argentina and Uruguay in colonial and early Republican days. But Blacks have been absorbed in many of these places and others, such as Chile, primarily through the process of "ethnic lynching." The non-white population even in Puerto Rico and Cuba has steadily decreased during the past two centuries, dropping from more than half the population to approximately one-fourth in both countries. Black Brazilians too are being "forced to acculturate, assimilate, to enter the world of whiteness. . . ."*

Widespread miscegenation in Latin America . . . is a dubious sign of racial tolerance. Racial blending does not necessarily mean an absence of racial prejudice. More precisely: "It is an open question whether a society that sees every addition of white blood as a step toward purification is more, or less, prejudiced than a society that sees any appreciable trace of Negro blood as a mark of degradation."† In Latin America, then, where ethnic lynching can be considered "a manifestation of latent or camouflaged prejudice against Blacks,"‡ racial mixing goes in the

---

*Abdias do Nascimento, "Afro-Brazilian Culture," *Black Images* 1, nos. 3 and 4 (Autumn and Winter 1972), 42.

†David Brian Davis, *The Problem of Slavery in Western Culture* (Ithaca, N.Y.: Cornell University Press, 1966), p. 275.

‡Harry Hoetink, *Slavery and Race Relations in the Americas* (New York: Harper & Row, 1973), p. 156.

direction of a gradual whitening of the population and a corresponding reduction of "Black" blood until it becomes an infinitesimal drop. The expectation that ethnic lynching will eventually lead to the disappearance of Blacks presupposes the superiority of white over Black, and as such is a form of white racism.*

Ethnic lynching, with its implied acceptance of the superiority of whites over Blacks, suggests that aesthetic prejudice lies at the heart of the crisis of Black identity in Latin America. Aesthetic prejudice and the premium it places on whiteness, is, to be sure, responsible for the fact that African features decrease chances for social acceptance and ascent in Latin America. The argument that aesthetic prejudice in Latin America favors those who most approximate whiteness is advanced even by a young Japanese in Brazil, who said: "In my opinion race prejudice does not exist in Brazil; there exists an aesthetic prejudice. The Japanese who most resemble individuals of the white race—for example, one who has less elongated eyes—is better accepted."†...

While anti-Black prejudice is practiced both in Anglo and in Latin America, the singling out of Black people almost exclusively as special targets for racist treatment in Latin America indicates that the anti-Black aesthetic is perhaps the most obvious, though the least stressed, factor that differentiates the nature of the color problem in Latin America from the race issue in the United States.

---

*Roger Bastide, "Variations on Negritude," in *Negritude: Essays and Studies*, ed. Albert H. Barrian and Richard A. Long (Hampton, Va.: Hampton Institute Press, 1967), p. 71.

†H. Hoetink, *The Two Variants in Caribbean Race Relations: A Contribution to the Sociology of Segmented Societies* (London: Oxford University Press, 1967), p. 171.

Anti-African prejudice is a common denominator in race relations on both sides of the border. But whereas in the United States, color—that is, race prejudice—is directed not only toward all obviously Black people, but toward all people with "Black" blood as well, regardless of skin shade, in Latin America we have a color spectrum, and racist attitudes there are directed largely toward those colored people closer to the Black end of this spectrum. . . .

When we speak of race relations in Latin America, we must speak of black, brown and white relations. In the United States, we can use Black, or Afro-American, or any of the other terms in a collective sense to include those people, regardless of how white they may appear, who have the proverbial drop of "Black" blood. Thus, the simple Black–white polarity. Either one is Black or one is white. But not so in Latin America, where racial appearance, including color, and not the drop of blood, determines one's status, where a Black, once he becomes mixed, ceases to be rigidly classified with Black people as long as he possesses some "white" features, as long as he moves away, in appearance, from the Black end of the color spectrum. . . .

The "Black" drop of blood, then, does not pollute or contaminate in modern Latin America. Unlike in the past when the early immigrants—the "old Christians"— from Spain and Portugal placed great importance on racial "purity" or unpolluted whiteness, there is no longer a widespread objection or pathological reaction to a "touch of the tarbrush." People with brown skin are now aesthetically pleasing to the Latin American eye, even preferred as an aesthetic ideal. The preference for the *morena*, a brown-skinned woman, at least as an ideal sexual partner, is almost legendary in Brazil, where one of the hit songs back in the late Forties was "A Mulata é a tal," which means "the Mulatto girl is tops." Even the "somatic norm image," as Hoetink[*] has shown, is darker in the Latin countries. But Blackness is still a stigma, just as much, if not more, in Latin America as in the United States, especially when accompanied by other African characteristics and features further separating Blacks and whites. . . .

Language concepts in Latin America . . . have propagated, as in the United States, stereotyped thinking about Black people. Ann Cook,[†] one of the many Blacks from the United States who have traveled through Latin America only to return disillusioned with the reluctance to identify with Black there, encountered much anti-Black consciousness reflected in directly translatable phrases that are so much a part of the culture in the United States. Whether the language of the countries she visited was English, French, Spanish, Dutch, or Portuguese, she found that there were phrases for "good hair," or for "marrying light to improve the race," and others we would recognize immediately.

She writes too of the extreme consciousness of color she found in Brazil, where Euro-Brazilians, like many caucasian Latin Americans, claim to be colorblind. In Brazil she found that the more caucasoid a person looks the more readily he will boast to a Black foreigner of his Black blood. . . .

The author recounts other manifestations of anti-African, or anti-Black complex in Brazil, where the crisis of Black identity is compounded by those who try to minimize African features. Among her accounts is the story

---

[*]See his two books, *The Two Variants in Caribbean Race Relations* and *Slavery and Race Relations in the Americas*.

[†]Ann Cook, "Black Pride—Some Contradictions," *Negro Digest* 19 (February 1970), 36–42, 59–63.

of the obviously African woman who for four months lay in the hospital after seriously burning her skin trying to bleach herself with a soda solution. This woman, a brilliant young economist with very black skin, ordered a car completely white inside and out. She now goes around, Cook tells us, wearing a blond wig and with face powered white.*

The "bleaching" episode recounted by Ann Cook is a classic representation of the emphasis on racial appearance.... The other Ann Cook episode, however, it should be emphasized, suggests not only a manifestation of anti-Black complex in Brazil but also a tendency to admit Black blood only so long as it is not readily visible—in other words, a tendency toward a conditional admission of Black blood....

Historical pressures of white racism have forced an identity crisis on Black people in Latin America reminiscent of the color situation in the United States years ago when light-skinned Blacks, for the most part, turned their backs on their darker brothers. Blacks generally see themselves differently now in the United States, although there are some who still resent being referred to as Black. Regardless of their insistence, however, on seeing the word as a color rather than as a shared experience, a light skin in the United States is no longer significant to Black people....

Theoretically, pure Black people can take the great leap upward in Latin America, once they meet certain requirements. According to an old saying, and to recent popular thought and theory, a Black man can become white or be considered white like his light-skinned brother once he improves himself through financial, educational, or some

---

*Ibid., p. 41.

other means that hopefully will allow him to overcome the stigma of Blackness. However, contrary to this belief, on this point many Latin American writers, Black and white, concur: as far as the white man is concerned, a Black man's high rank, financial position, or superb personal qualifications do not necessarily improve his image, even if his wealth or power is accepted and his Blackness politely ignored. . . .

The "etiquette of race relations"* is a major obstacle to the achievement of a real racial democracy and an impediment to the full recognition of the rights and privileges of Blacks in *mestizo* societies. The etiquette of race relations, in effect, places a moratorium on the discussion, certainly the admission, of the existence of prejudice and discrimination. An effective camouflage is the use of Blacks who have "made it," such as Pelé the king of football (soccer) in Brazil, to demonstrate the validity of racial-democracy propaganda. Government attempts to forbid denunciation of the racial-democracy myth in Brazil, as well as the official attempts to mask the serious problems and to silence the voices of those who would rise up to denounce racism, are called "white magic"† by Abdias do Nascimento.

Yet no amount of "white washing" can erase the fact that in Latin America today the Black man's biggest fight is still against racism and the white aesthetic, or that it is expected that it is he who, in the interest of racial peace, will eventually disappear from *mestizo* societies. And while the complete range of racial mores and attitudes toward race

---

*A phrase used by Anani Dzidzienyo in *The Position of Blacks in Brazilian Society* (London: Minority Rights Group Report, 1971), no. 7, p. 5.
†"Afro-Brazilian Culture," *Black Images* nos. 3 and 4 (Autumn and Winter, 1972), 42.

and color prevalent in the United States might not exist in Latin America, the massive program deemed necessary in the United States for "deconditioning" people from the white-superior, Black-inferior syndrome would not be totally irrelevant if applied as well to Latin America, where black skin and African features continue to be handicaps, white racism and anti-Black consciousness realities, and ethnic lynching a serious threat to the racial identity of Black people—indeed, to their very existence as a distinct race with its own Black aesthetic.

25.
Niani (Dee Brown), "Black Consciousness vs. Racism in Brazil"

Deloris A. Brown is an attorney and freelance writer who lives in Los Angeles. She served as a Peace Corps volunteer in northeastern Brazil from 1964 to 1967 and has returned frequently to that area since then. She has also written about Afro-Brazil in "Bahia: The City of All Saints," Uraeus 2 *(Winter 1980), 5–10.*

Introduction

WE AFRICAN-AMERICANS, having recently begun to enjoy some of the economic benefits not here-to-fore possible are traveling in droves to other countries and for the first time are beginning to interchange with other Africans living in other parts of the world. We take with us many experiences; they can benefit from us and in turn, we learn ourselves. In a recent trip back to Brazil, I was fortunate to have met with a group of Brazilian brothers and sisters involved in a movement which may possibly have a devastating effect on the Brazilian political scene.

The United Black Movement Against Racial Discrimi-

From *The Black Scholar* 11 (January/February 1980), 59–70. Reprinted by permission of *The Black Scholar*, Oakland, California.

nation (MNU) is this new and potentially explosive force. Although less than two years old, the MNU has mobilized thousands of persons—students, professionals, artists—in nationwide protest demonstrations, and conferences focusing on the problem of racial discrimination and police violence against them.

To date its activities have served to stimulate unusual political discussion among the general urban populace about the racial problem though to a large extent, society continues to ignore or negate the existence of this problem. Nevertheless, during its first year of existence, the MNU has fostered a new racial consciousness and pride among a small but well-organized segment of the Afro-Brazilian population. Since the importance of the United Black Movement could easily equal that of the U.S. black freedom movement of the 60s, it behooves us to study closely its development.

The basis of this movement is a history of racial and class oppression of the Afro-Brazilian which in some respects parallels our own. Brazil's solution to the race problem has been to follow a policy of "miscegenation" (i.e. of racial mixing), to the extent that the question becomes one of "color" rather than "race" per se. Failure of this policy of miscegenation is most probably one of the key factors giving rise to this "Black Movement." If so, the Brazilian social model may give us some indication as to how to, or how not to, guide our own struggle.

Miscegenation: Answer to the Race Question?

One of the factors that differentiates racism as a dynamic in Brazil from that in the United States is that extensive racial mixing has occurred between the European, indigenous or Amerindian peoples and the African slave. This practice of the Portuguese was not conscious in terms of social policy so much as race apparently was much less important a factor in the cultural-social development of Brazil than it was in this country. As a result, African culture became thoroughly integrated into what can be recognized as the "Brazilian" culture.

After their emancipation, blacks became political pawns in the political process during which the country was beginning to change from an imperial to a republican regime. A predominant school of thought developed which tried to minimize any idea of race consciousness.

This "melting pot" concept accomplished an important, evolving national purpose: primarily, blacks were given to de-emphasize any racial, cultural distinctions; corollary to this came an elaborate and confusing classification scheme based on skin coloring and to a degree, social status. At the same time an "Aryan" position developed as a means of justifying Brazil's inferiority or lack of technological progress internationally.

One spokesman of this school of thought, Vianna Olivera [Oliveira Vianna], articulated the concept which stated that Brazil's deficiencies as a nation resulted from the "inferiority of the racial mixture," i.e. miscegenation. He pointed out the inability of Afro-Brazilians to assimilate into a basically European culture. He further explained that the blacks' mentality, being different from that of whites, resulted in their maladjustment to the dominant European mode. But he emphasized, the black is *culturally*, not racially, inferior. Pro-Aryan thought, exemplified in the culture, literature, philosophy and jurisprudence of that time, served to mute abolitionist tendencies.

Anti-Aryan spokesmen, Gilberto Freyre[1] and Arthur

Ramos,[2] offered the view that the Brazilian racial mixture made for a creative, intelligent and capable people. This attitude accepted the inevitability of racial mixing, which had been in evidence since the first coming of the Portuguese. It was "sympathizers" holding these ideas who supported the abolition of slavery and successfully advocated emancipation.

However, the miscegenation idea was ironically based on the notion that the greater the incidence of racial mixing, the closer to a pure white society, hence an adequate resolution of the race question. This idea led to the concept known as the Brazilian "Social Democracy," implying that Brazil has discovered an ideal social model resulting in racial harmony. While serving Brazil's interests internationally, this concept has been used effectively as an excuse for not meeting the needs of the black population.

Though there existed no equivalent to societal racial segregation or physical lynchings to characterize the Brazilian post-emancipation period, a more subtle form of racial oppression began to take shape. Notwithstanding legal equality, masked social discrimination prevailed and continues to dominate as a national attitude throughout Brazil, particularly in urban centers which are characterized by a highly economically competitive environment.

It has been said that there are at least 40 different "racial" classifications for individuals depending on one's hair texture and shade, lip width, and skin tone.* To further add to this complicated and confusing system of identification, the more education and money one attains, the "whiter" he becomes! So that it is possible for a person

---

*Marvin Harris, *Patterns of Race in the Americas* (New York: Walker & Co., 1964), p. 58.

to pass through several categories in a short span of time. Thus, it is for this reason that certain socio-anthropologists are quick to point out that race is only one of several factors which may determine discriminatory treatment. To simplify the identification process, the official categories used are white (*branco*), brown or mixed (*pardo*), and black (*preto*).

While it is true that, comparatively speaking, social relationships in Brazil are characterized more along class lines than in the United States, it is also true that the lowest social-economic class is unquestionably "black." Also evident throughout the society is the emphasis given to European values as being superior, hence they are the most coveted values.

This trend is by no means coincidental but rather is characteristic of a social, as well as political, policy which is at best patronizing, at worst, discriminatory against African values and social patterns. By regarding the color problem as one of "class" instead of race, the government can effectively ignore the lack of social and economic opportunity of Afro-Brazilians as a social group. Not only has this policy officially absolved the government from its inaction, but virtually all Brazilians, including blacks, adhere to the official whitening process as a means of improving their condition.

Since the "Golden Law" of abolition,[3] the government has had to pass only one law, i.e. the Afonso Arinos Law against racial discrimination in public accommodations. This law was enacted in 1951 shortly after Katherine Dunham, the celebrated black American dancer, was refused accommodation at one of the hotels in Rio de Janeiro while on a dance tour. Although the law is still on the books, little effort has been made to effectively enforce it.

The Brazilian consciousness idea in its practical aspects is depicted in Gilberto Freyre's book *Order and Progress*.* He tells about a cadre of expert *capoeira*† fighters known as The Black Guard recognized for their fierce fighting abilities, who rallied to defend the empire against "republican" agitators during the last days of Don Pedro II.‡

They were employed by imperial politicos as personal body guards while their actions in using the deadly fighting technique were decried as being "disgraceful." As a result, after the republic was established, "capoeiristas" (persons practicing capoeira) were persecuted. This persecution was claimed not to be racially inspired but rather to be persecution of those who were anti-republicans. Freyre notes that it would have been more useful to the government armed forces to have adopted this form of unique fighting instead of negating it.

Afro-Brazilians—An Economic Problem

After May 13, 1888, date of the Brazilian emancipation, the country struggled through an economic crisis as a result of not having adequately prepared for the blow emancipation gave to what was mainly an agrarian society. The agricultural upheaval was blamed on the government's lack of foresight in anticipating the need for drastic economic change. Capital funds began to shift from the

---

*Gilberto Freyre is a noted Brazilian social anthropologist who has written several important works describing the social situation between the races.

†Capoeira is a method of fighting with the legs and feet, developed by the slaves when anything that could be used as a weapon was taken away from them. It is practiced as a dance form principally in Bahia.

‡Don Pedro II was the last monarch of the Portuguese to reign over Brazil prior to formation of the republic.

north to the south around 1860, in a prospective need to diversify Brazil's one-crop sugar economy.

São Paulo, the southern, highly industrialized state, was established as a center of national economy where coffee replaced sugar as the leading agricultural product. São Paulo also began to produce materials and products which competed well with foreign imports. Merger of the Bank of Brazil with the Bank of the Republic increased money supply in the form of loans which aided states in both agricultural as well as industrial projects.

European and black immigration to São Paulo increased as a result of the developing and prosperous coffee industry. This period was particularly hard on the ex-slave who, much like the North American freedman, possessed few of the skills needed to compete effectively within the new economic order.

Under the slave economy, most blacks were used primarily as beasts of burden, although many who learned trade skills were hired out by their masters as streetpavers, boatmen, blacksmiths, printers, gardeners, hairdressers, and carpenters. After emancipation, these ex-slaves were able to utilize their skills as "free workers." Gradually slave labor was replaced with labor of free workers, a process which began even before emancipation. So widespread was this practice in Bahia* that by 1870 an organization—a precursor to modern day labor unions—was formed employing free workers in manual activity for legitimate wages.

The need for vocational training became apparent as

---

*Bahia is the northeastern state and city characterized by its strong African influence.

the most effective way to develop this neglected human resource. Schools began to appear in major cities. The School of Arts and Trades was established in Rio in 1878 and by 1880, the number of students, both national and foreign, rose from 1,049 to 1,341.

Such schools offered instruction in printing, bookbinding, tailoring and musical instruction. Since government projects of engineering, sanitation and hygiene called for vast numbers of trained technicians, several institutions of a technical nature were established at the university level in the states of Minas Gerais, Rio de Janeiro and Bahia.

Military service was a primary means of upgrading black Brazilians socially and economically around the late 1880s. While their white counterparts progressed socially by studying law or medicine, the "mestiço"* or "mulatto" gained prestige in the military. Military schools also fed, clothed and educated the socially-upward black Brazilian.

The new technically trained university graduates emerged as a new elite class, displacing to a degree, the military elite who dominated the society at the beginning of the Republic. Gilberto Freyre notes that this period marked the beginning of what he refers to as a "proletarian consciousness" where representatives of the working classes began to appear in the state and national legislatures. And significantly enough, most of these men were mestizos or mulattos.

Myth of a Social Democracy

While coffee, rubber and maté (tea) propelled Brazil into the prominence of international trade, the Brazilian

---

*Mestiço [Mestizo] is a mixture of white and Indian.

culture was being propagandized as a "neo-European" culture. Brazil, anxious to change its "inferior" world image, rushed into industrialization as a means of "civilizing" itself. The accelerated push toward an industrialized society divulged great contradictions in the Brazilian social order in contrast to the national social philosophy of amalgamation. Examples of these contradictions are most blatantly seen in the developing urban areas of Rio and São Paulo.

As the ex-slaves migrated from the north to the south—primarily in search of work opportunities around the Rio and São Paulo areas—they brought with them a complex and conflicting value system and social rituals reminiscent of the U.S. southern plantation system in which the slaves were totally dependent upon their owners for survival. They tended to exhibit a docile, humble manner of behavior with respect to whites which worked against their advancement as a group in the competitive atmosphere. Likewise they carried with them an ambivalent attitude toward the utilization of their labor as a means of social progression.

In keeping with the official policy of "Order and Progress,"* patriotism to the idea of "one people" was spawned via the educational system. Children of both ex-slaves and European immigrants studied textbooks which taught that Brazil was the country of one's "ideals" though it might not be the country of one's birth or origin.

However, Europeans from Germany and Poland who immigrated to the southern states of Santa Catarina, São Paulo and Rio Grande do Sul, being less inclined to the as-

---

*This was also a motto adopted by the government for the Brazilian flag and was followed as a policy.

similation process, were able to continue as ethnic groups by voting as a bloc for governmental candidates. Except for the Italians, whose culture was similar to that of the Portuguese, European immigrants resisted the miscegenation process.

Emergence of the myth of Brazil as a "Social Democracy"* was seen as necessary to serve several official ends: first, it engendered a widespread attitude, both among black and white, that the problems of black urban population were due to their "incapacity and irresponsibility." It further exempted whites from moral responsibility in the progressive deterioration of the socio-economic situation of blacks. By presenting this false concept of racial relations, it created a standard for judging black–white relations by giving an external appearance of racial adjustment.

Certain Brazilian thinkers believe the perpetuation of the myth ultimately served to undermine any true tendency of democracy in social relationships by engendering the belief among blacks of their own "inferiority," i.e. that they can't be given any authority or responsibility and that they will only progress under the guidance of the superior white.†

In his book *The Negro in the Brazilian Society*, a case study of socio-economic influences on blacks, Florestan Fernandes points out three essential dynamics which occurred in São Paulo at the turn of the century. First, slave labor was shifted from the city to the prosperous agricultural areas of the interior; second, the migration of freed

---

*The phrase "social democracy" was coined by Gilberto Freyre.
†Florestan Fernandes, *The Negro in Brazilian Society* (New York: Columbia University Press, 1969), p. 144.

blacks to the cities seeking job opportunities; and third, the rapid increase in white population due to a large-scale settlement of immigrants to the city. Between 1872 and 1886, 31 percent of the population increase in the white segment was due to growth of native stock while 69 percent was due to European immigration.[*]

The impact of economic competition on freed blacks proved overwhelming as they lacked the means to defend the prior advantageous positions they had acquired. White immigrants, on the other hand, competed successfully for jobs with specialized skills in occupations essential to rapid urban expansion and industrialization. Former slave labor was relegated to occupations that were marginal or accessory to capitalist production, or to such essential services for which there were no white workers available, e.g. garbagemen, janitors, clerks, domestics, office boys.[†]

As white Brazilians had little to fear from blacks by way of economic or political competition, no racial hatred or intolerance developed as did during the U.S. Reconstruction period. The old order of race relations which protected and preserved white superiority was favored and was maintained. Blacks, on the other hand, generally accepted this paternalistic attitude. According to the findings in the Fernandes study, the social attitude toward blacks was covert and based on distrust.

Although rejected and despised secretly, blacks were openly accepted—but not without restrictions. A government decree of June 28, 1890, reflected a liberal immigration policy which openly invited European immigrants to the country for work, yet supported the national goal of whitening the population by restricting immigrants from

[*] Ibid., p. 11.
[†] Ibid., p. 76.

Asia or Africa. An ambivalent pattern of rejection of trends to treat blacks as equals emerged, while at the same time their newly found juridico-political position was accepted.

The impact of social interaction between blacks and whites within the new social order led Fernandes to several conclusions. First, the existence of interracial contacts and relationships were a deception of the reality of masked, rigid and insurmountable racial inequality.

Secondly, a dichotomy between the prevailing white social order and aspirations of blacks toward upward mobility established a new pattern of operating within the culture. This meant that to achieve a certain social status—given no segregated black society existed—blacks had to blend into the various levels of lower and middle classes of the dominant racial group. But their undistinguishable racial characteristics determinably relegated them to an inferior status by members of the dominant group.

Thirdly, social position and skin coloring were linked in such a way that the more closely one resembled those persons of the "subordinate" racial group, the more likely that person was discriminated against, notwithstanding the degree of his or her social advancement. Thus racial characteristics of the dominant group were prerogatives to privileges of the social elite.

Fourthly, the social distance between the races, which caused unequal social treatment, was constantly assaulted by blacks themselves who in certain instances demanded identical treatment to that granted members of the dominant race.

Fifth, the possibly upward mobility by a few blacks proved insufficient in creating any permanent change in race relations. This was due in part to the inability of "vertical mobile members" to express their dissatisfaction as a constructive and autonomous social force, i.e. expressing a perception of reality *outside* and *apart* from that of the dominant group.

Finally, the slow discontinuous development of the competitive social order served to perpetuate the old order of asymmetric race relations, which in turn governed the process of redefining the blacks' image. Hence, traditional paternalistic patterns of race relations were reinforced, perpetuating the inferior status of the black position within the society.

Having no institutions to help them in this transition, blacks were forced to accept socially degrading conditions. Opportunities, which were few and far between, however, were based not only on skills, but on "coloring" as well. Social stigma and the lack of economic means to defend themselves as a group, created a tendency toward isolation from the socio-cultural forces that identified them as slaves! This "disassociation" was seen as a necessary means of entry into the Brazilian class system.

Urban living forced blacks to change many of their traditions, customs and social patterns. The difficulty in adjusting to this new social arrangement was brought about by an inability to comprehend the social dynamics of a European oriented society.

When cultural practices such as religious drumming were prevented by the police or otherwise looked upon with disdain by the dominant community to the point of abandonment, these cultural losses were not compensated for. Consequently, exclusion on even superficial levels of activities basic to urbanization created not only the phenomenon of social isolationism but also began a pattern of *disorganization* within the black social system similar in many of its aspects to the North American black urban experience.

It became easier for women to find jobs than for men, particularly in the domestic service areas. Eventually, prompted by a scarcity of workers, black women found new opportunities in such fields as dressmaking, embroidery, bookbinding, etc. These new roles for women and men combined with other social pressures to change their patterns of interrelating to each other.

Occasional work and erratic earnings led the men to such a state of dependence and hardship that women became their principal resource in the struggle of existence. This dependence led to systematic exploitation, a situation which became socially acceptable and continues today. Forced idleness and vagrancy turned into a permanent way of life for men who were demoralized to the point of accepting their condition. It was either this or resort to a way of crime.

Unmarried mothers worked at whatever they could find, leaving their children with neighbors to watch or to fend for themselves. When the women were unable to find work, they resorted to begging or street prostitution. Their children were called "street urchins," earning money at an early age by running errands or by begging. In time a whole mythology circulated both inside the "ghetto" as well as within the general community.

Crowded housing conditions, of several persons living in single-room occupancy, forced people out into the streets and resulted in increased sexual activity for those unemployed. Pathological consequences, of poor hygienic conditions, unemployment, sexual exploitation and general social anomie led to criminal activity, alcoholism, disease, abandoned children, homosexuality and other sexually deviant behavior. Not only did these conditions bring about the breakdown of the black family unit, but class divisions resulted between these and other blacks fortunate enough to achieve economic and social parity with whites.

Blacks who had adopted the white man's morality and social ideals despised the others whom they considered irresponsible, not wanting to "get ahead." They saw in the brothers and sisters of inferior position a threat to their own prestige, which depended on how the "white man" perceived them.

This small and relatively exclusive segment of the black population withdrew both from the urban black lower class as well as from the behavior of foreign whites or large landowners, striving to create a destiny of their own. They saw the need for having to prove themselves in order to survive; the need for resolving their own problems in accordance with the ethical-juridical code established by society. This meant they had a choice of either assimilating the cultural techniques, patterns of living and social values upon which patterns were based, or remaining chained to the same conditions that stigmatized them as societal psychopaths.

Organized Black Efforts

By the 1930s, a conventional expectation of stereotypic behavior provided a convenient frame of reference for understanding what was considered to be the human nature of the black Brazilian. From 1925 to 1930 dissatisfaction of the black population had grown to such a degree that several spontaneous movements developed representing a growing awareness and criticism of the destiny to which they were relegated.

Afro-Brazilians had, since the abolitionist movement, participated actively in organized activities for their liberation, often times collaborating with whites. Two significant conferences having cultural objectives were held in the northeastern cities of Recife, Pernambuco (1934) and Salvador, Bahia (1937).* On the other hand, organized efforts in São Paulo took on more political tones, their examples spreading elsewhere, where later organizations patterned similar objectives.

In the city of São Paulo, a handful of persons managed to overcome the apathy caused by social disintegration to convince blacks to cooperate collectively for their own benefit. They tried to bring together the mulatto and the "negro" in an effort which fostered a new attitude that oriented integrationist and assimilationist aspirations in the direction of egalitarian demands.

Group objectives which were expounded and disseminated through the *Clarim da Alvorada*, an influential publication of the movement, were influenced by observing the success foreign groups attained through organized forms. Basic goals were to improve the civil, moral and intellectual conditions of the race through a re-educational process. In line with these goals several clubs were formed serving literary, social and recreational purposes. At times mass support was mobilized around isolated incidents of discrimination, bringing the black population directly into the political process.

*These Congresses sought to document the contribution of African influences on the Brazilian culture. Only residually did they push the equality issue, and this was in the demand for recognition of the African sects as valid religious practice.

In 1931, a politically oriented group called *Frente Negra Brasileira* (FNB) (Black Front) was organized as a direct result of this preliminary effort. The FNB operated both as a political force, intending the election of state representatives, and as a social movement providing for the "intellectual, artistic, technical, professional and physical" needs of its members. As such it organized funds for the poor, gave aid to women, encouraged educational achievement and interracial understanding, and lobbied the government to establish free tuition for blacks at the university level.

The Front's own newspaper, *A Voz da Raça* (Voice of the Race) was utilized as a tool for proselytizing its theme of self-determination and achievement. Basically, it can be characterized as forging an assimilationist social movement encouraging behavior patterns which would speed up the process of integration of blacks into the class society.

Whatever contributions the Front made were effectively terminated in 1936 under the New State (Estado Novo) regime of President Getúlio Vargas who executed a bloodless coup in 1930. Having been successfully organized into a political party, the Front was outlawed along with all other parties. Attempts at reorganization under a new name proved unsuccessful.

MNU: A New Means of Protest

In order to more fully understand the political dynamics within which the MNU operates, a brief overview of the political-economic climate in which it was born is necessary. The international trend of social consciousness which characterized the 60s also found expression in Brazil. Feeling an ideological alliance with their counterparts in the

U.S. protesting Vietnam, Brazilian students organized a movement to denounce repressive government policies.

Since the 1964 coup in which army general Castello Branco took over the reins of power, civil liberties have given way to a centralization of power—particularly in the Presidency—for the sake of stabilizing an uncontrollable inflation-ridden economy. Initially, the military take-over had popular support; the masses seeing it as having the means to halt the political corruption and to reverse the worsening economic conditions.

Fearing an impending social change, the ruling elite supported the military, giving it a mandate to "preserve the liberal ideal" by whatever measures it saw necessary. Thus any political action was viewed as a threat to a stable Brazil, meaning no such action was permitted. However, public pressure from various sectors of the society has succeeded in pushing the government, since the '67 Costa e Silva regime, to permitting individual and group political expression.

The U.S. Civil Rights Movement, particularly the concept of "Black Power," apparently had a significant impact on the growing black Brazilian consciousness. The cultural climate had always been fertile for the idea of black pride, but to openly embrace such a concept brought about social ridicule, given the myth of the "social democracy." Still many white Brazilians sympathetic to the black movement caution against the dangers of creating a movement which may lead to racial separatism.

In early May 1978, in São Paulo, a black worker, Robson Silveira da Luz, was beaten to death by the police while being held in detention. May 17, 1978, four young black athletes were expelled from a volleyball team of the Regatas Tiete Club of São Paulo strictly because they were black. July 1, 1978, Nilton Lourenco, a black factory worker, was killed by the police in a suburb of São Paulo. As a result of these events a public demonstration was held July 7 to protest the pattern of police violence and racial discrimination against Afro-Brazilians. More than 1,000 persons participated in the demonstration held on the steps of the Municipal Theater of São Paulo.

Since July 18 (official date of birth of the MNU), its idea has grown nationally through a series of meetings, the first occurring July 23, 1978, in São Paulo. At this meeting the group established an interstate and intrastate communications and organizational structure, and adopted several items to work on until the first national assembly could be called.

On September 9 and 10, 1978, MNU representatives from several states met in Rio to approve an action program, Charter of Principles, and By-laws. As a basic principle, the organization recognizes those persons as black who "possess Black racial characteristics and hair texture." It acknowledges that such persons have suffered racial discrimination in the form of unemployment and underemployment; economic and social marginalization; police and political repression and persecution; sexual, social, economical exploitation of black women; commercialization and colonization of culture; sub-human conditions and treatment of black prisoners; sub-human living conditions . . . all existing under the myth of "racial democracy."

Resolutions were made to directly address these problems by concerted action. Other basic adopted goals were that this struggle should be led only by blacks; that a "new society" should be one in which all persons would participate.

The MNU Action Program comprises the following

nine areas: (1) against racial discrimination in employment, living conditions, and in the health care areas; (2) against racial discrimination in prisons; (3) against discrimination in education; (4) against commercialization and distortion of black culture; (5) against systematic forms of oppression, persecution and police violence; (6) for the right to equal access at recreational and social places, and in public accommodations; (7) for the full participation of the women in the struggle for black liberation; (8) for solidarity in the international struggle against racism—supporting liberation struggles in Namibia, Zimbabwe and "South Africa"; (9) for the freedom of political organizing and expression of black people—including the right to organize "Fighting Centers" in all locales within the black community; to reconstruct the black press; and the right for illiterates to vote.

Organization is the key to the limited success the MNU has had up to now. To this end, it has organized cell groups called "Fighting Centers" (Centros de Luta) through which its activities are directed. These "centers"—established in all major social, cultural, educational, even work locations—educate and mobilize the masses around issues of local concern as well as around police killings and mistreatment of black citizens.

Essential to achieving MNU goals, education of the masses is continuously being done via the circulation of "public letters" which focus on the problems of racism in general as evidenced in the nine areas of the Action Program. In each letter, specific incidents of known discriminatory acts are reiterated, emphasizing the need for widespread support of the MNU program.

Realizing the need to create a positive way to express African culture, and in keeping with the spirit of creating a new society, November 20, 1978, was celebrated by the MNU as National Day of Black Conscientiousness. Honor was given to Zumbi, leader of the Black Republic of Palmares.* This day, date of Zumbi's death, is recognized by the MNU to replace May 13, the date of the Emancipation, as the date of black liberation.

In general, public reaction to the MNU has been suspicious. The Brazilian press for the most part, keeping in line with its policy of supporting the need for greater political freedom of expression, has readily printed the organization's press releases and has given widespread coverage to its public demonstrations. The government, surprisingly, has not taken any extreme steps to curtail its operation. However, group members are undoubtedly kept under surveillance and all activities are carefully monitored.

An incident which occurred December 2, 1978, may indicate the policy which the government has decided to take with respect to the MNU. This particular Friday evening, at one of the student centers on the Campinas State University campus in São Paulo, a "samba" dance, held after a MNU meeting, was stopped by the military police.† The police, who alleged that a criminal suspect was among the MNU group, began assaulting both men and women alike with clubs and racial slurs. Finally, 24 persons were arrested, taken to the local precinct where they were made to disrobe pending identification. The MNU, along with other student groups, have protested this action.

Looking toward the possibility of forming a political

---

*Palmares was a black independent nation established in the state of Alagoas from 1595 to 1695, which was formed by escaped slaves, and which successfully defended itself against Portuguese and Dutch attempts to overthrow it.

†Being a military dictatorship, Brazilian military—while highly visible—are generally the enforcement authority of last resort.

party, the MNU has already taken steps in this direction. A second National Assembly was held November 4, 1978, in Salvador, Bahia, to influence the black electorate for the national elections held November 1978. At this assembly certain opposition party* candidates were officially criticized for soft-pedaling the "race" question, while four candidates running for Federal Senatorial seats were supported. Election results showed the Movimento Democrático Brasileira (MDB) gaining more seats than ever before, since the military take-over of government! Of the four MNU candidates, one was elected!

Conclusion

The success of MNU efforts may well depend on the degree to which African-Brazilians recognize themselves as being "black." Certainly no degree of unity will be achieved where a black population doesn't perceive itself as such.

On the other hand, MNU's political skill, particularly in the international arena, may render the "black unity" of less importance. MNU leaders, for instance, believe that the organization's activities have thus far been tolerated by the restrictive military government mainly because of the government's reluctance to openly acknowledge the problem and risk tarnishing Brazil's international reputation of having achieved an ideal social model. Nevertheless, there exist many obstacles to such unity; historical, social, as well as geographical.

Tolerance by the Brazilian government of increased

---

*Of the two parties in Brazil, the MDB (Movimento Democratico Brasileira) is the official opposition party.

political expression by such groups cannot be overlooked as another key factor in determining the extent of the MNU's impact. This consideration, compared to the group's internal organizational problems, is paramount and more difficult to assess.

The feasible idea of creating a black political party could be thwarted again as occurred under the Vargas regime. Yet if a substantial majority of the black population were organized into one political force, such repressive action may prove to have disastrous effects. To counteract this possible domestic political strategy the MNU may have to seek support from outside the country!

By virtue of its large population of African descent— about 60 percent of a population of 80 million—Brazil stands out as a country for us to take interest in. Indeed the degree of our concern with the problems and struggles of all African peoples in the Americas may play an important part in their own struggles.

I have heard it said more than once by young militant Brazilian brothers that the U.S. Black Power Movement was the key to giving a resurgence to this, the newest of Afro-Brazilian political movements. These brothers and sisters are anxious to exchange ideas and knowledge with us in the United States so that through the sharing of mutual experiences we both may gain insight and strength in our struggle.

NOTES

1. Freyre was a Brazilian social historian who, in such works as *The Masters and the Slaves* (1933) and *The Mansions and the Shanties* (1933), emphasized the African influence in

Brazilian culture and the benign nature of slavery under the Portuguese. He was the leading proponent of the concept of the Brazilian "social democracy."

2. Ramos was a Brazilian psychiatrist and anthropologist who wrote a number of books on Afro-Brazilians.

3. The law of May 13, 1888, granted unconditional freedom to all slaves in Brazil.

26.

Gloria Calomee, "Brazil and the Blacks of South America"

Gloria Calomee lives in Los Angeles where she works as a producer, writer, and actress. Her travel articles and essays on Third World arts and artists have appeared in the Los Angeles Times, Cinephile Magazine, *and* Neworld Magazine.

THE WORLD may see Brazil as a "colored" nation today, but the Brazilian government would prefer that the world see her differently, . . . as a white nation with a flavoring added by an African-derived subculture. White Brazil promotes a racial classification/separation system among Afro-Brazilians (as do whites throughout most of Latin America) which so far has worked to the detriment of Afro-Brazilians insofar as their economic, social and political status within the society. At the top of the classification system are whites, a class by themselves; under them is the African-derived subculture, broken down as follows: mulatto, cafuso [a person of mixed Amerindian and African ancestry], black (in that order of importance).

From *The Crisis* 93 (June/July 1986), pp. 37, 38, 40, 58, 61. Reprinted by permission of the Crisis Publishing Co., New York, New York.

One might think that this classification system is based on actual skin color (sometimes it is, sometimes it isn't; sometimes it is simply based on the amount of money one earns). If one is dark but has some economic standing, one could have the dubious honor of being labeled mulatto. If one is relatively light-skinned, but poor, that person could be considered cafuso or even black. There are as many definitions as there are definers. Show any two Brazilians the same photo of an Afro-Brazilian family, one person might see two racial groups in the photo, the other three. Show a Brazilian a photo of a black Brazilian and caption the photo with the information that the person is a doctor, and he will probably be labeled mulatto. Change the caption to laborer, and he would then most probably be labeled black. The bi-racial attitude that exists in the States (if one is of African descent one is black; of one is not of African descent, one is not black) is rigidly opposed here, especially by the white power structure, for their type of classification means separation, and separation means disunity. In this nation of more than 60 percent blacks (people of African descent), one can see how it is in the best interests of the white power structure to promote a system that ensures disunity among Afro-Brazilians.

As a result of white Brazil's promotion of this system of classification, Afro-Brazilians seem to be stuck in a sort of pre-racial pride and unity incubation period. Black Americans who remember the 60s and the "black is beautiful" movement might also remember what went on prior to that period. "Light-skinned" blacks "passed" for white; there was the "paper-bag" test (one couldn't get into certain "Negro" clubs or organizations if one was not the color of the paper bag or lighter), and people still spoke of such things as "good hair." But the liberation movements changed all that. Black Brazil is still stuck in pre-60s mentality . . . to be black is bad, to be mulatto is better, to be white is best of all.

Mulatto is an interesting word, albeit an antiquated one here in the States. It was utilized here mostly in the south, especially in the French and Spanish colonies of Louisiana and Florida. Mulatto meant very specifically half white and half African. But that definition died fairly rapidly as any real indication of race; for it seems to have worked to our benefit, having produced a racial unity which doesn't seem to exist amongst blacks elsewhere in the Americas.

Black playwright, artist and now Senator Abdias do Nascimento dealt with this theme in his haunting play "Sortilegio," which was first performed at his Teatro do Negro in Rio de Janeiro in the 1950s and at the Inner City Cultural Center in Los Angeles in 1975. The character Emanuel, a black physician, gives up his black lover Efigenia once he starts to climb the ladder of success and takes a white bride in order to help him improve his status in the society. His decision to cut his ties with his "blackness" haunts and torments him to the point of his destruction. Do Nascimento is one of only a few black voices coming out of Brazil today; he is also the only black representative in the Brazilian senate. The old axiom holds true in Brazil today: the poor and powerless are the darkest, the rich and powerful are the whitest. . . .

From music to religion to food, the African influence has left its mark on Brazil as well as on most of Latin America. Black Americans, as a result of racial unity, have made an impact not only on their own society but on the world. Aside from Desmond Tutu or Pelé (the only black soccer star to come out of Brazil, despite the many blacks who excel at the sport there), it has been the black American who is most visible. From King to Jackson, from Baldwin to Ali, from Belafonte to Wonder, what they do and say resounds around the world, and sometimes even makes a difference. But what our brothers and sisters in the rest of the Americas have is another kind of unity, based on cultural identity, that unbroken link with Africa which we are still struggling to re-connect. There are important lessons to be learned from each other.

A sampling of population figures for South America today (keeping in mind the fact that these are government figures and do not necessarily reflect accurately the black population) read: in Venezuela 31 to 40 percent of the population is black; in Ecuador 10 to 15 percent; in Brazil more than 60 percent, out of a total population of 160 million . . . which means that there are approximately over 100 million people of African descent in Brazil alone. If one were to add together all the figures from Latin America, the Caribbean and the U.S.A., it would be obvious that the combined influence of all Afro-Americans throughout the Americas could be a cultural and political force which would shape the future of a truly "New World."

27.

Rachel Jackson Christmas, "In Harmony with Brazil's African Pulse"

Rachel Jackson Christmas, a 1979 graduate of Wesleyan University, was a book editor for six years and is now a freelance writer. She is the co-author of Fielding's Bermuda and the Bahamas *and author of* Fielding's Hawaii.

As WE CLIMBED off a bus at the Barra Lighthouse in Salvador, the capital of Bahia in Brazil, several young boys, smiling broadly, chanted "Africa do Sul!" and held their fists in the air. I was among a group of African-American friends who might have blended in with Bahia's predominantly black population had it not been for our cameras and sightseeing attire. At first I thought the boys were proclaiming their support for the freedom of South Africa. It did not take me long to realize that what they were actually telling us was that Bahia was the Africa of South America.

We felt the African pulse in the beat of samba, known as semba in Angola; swallowed it with the spicy food, made with nuts, coconut milk, ginger and okra also used in

From *The New York Times*, Sunday, November 20, 1988, pp. xx, 43. Copyright © 1988 by The New York Times Company. Reprinted by permission.

African cooking; witnessed it in Candomblé ceremonies, rooted in the religion of the Yorubas of Nigeria; heard it in the musical Yoruban accent of the Portuguese spoken in the state of Bahia. This African heritage is an integral part of what it means to be Brazilian—black, white or in between.

Over the course of three hundred years, beginning in 1548, Portuguese colonists forced some five million West Africans into ships bound for Brazil, which drew almost 40 percent of the Atlantic slave trade, about seven times more than the United States. Families were torn apart and people from the same communities were separated. Yet these slaves, who were put to work on sugar plantations, held tenaciously to many aspects of the cultures they had left behind.

Today Bahians seem far more aware of their origins than African-Americans are. European- or Asian-Americans may not speak French or Gaelic or Cantonese, but they certainly know which countries their ancestors came from and can easily find out about their cultures. In both America and Brazil, European enslavers made sure that few black people today know exactly what country or tribe their predecessors came from. But, in part because of the concentration of slaves in Brazil, a life style incorporating elements of disparate African cultures developed and flourished there. Brazil's population is about 44 percent black and mixed race. Bahia's is more than 80 percent black.

I was not surprised at how refreshing it felt to be among people who were so firmly tethered to our common past. And though angered, I was not surprised by the all-too-familiar racial discrimination that—a century after the abolition of slavery—is still so apparent. Afro-Brazilian

"In Harmony with Brazil's African Pulse"

doctors, engineers and teachers earn 20 to 25 percent less than whites. And when job advertisements seek "people of good appearance" they mean people with white or light skin. What I didn't expect was to discover that perhaps my life had not been as removed from my African roots as I had thought.

In Salvador, the roller-coaster cobblestone streets provide an intriguing stage for an audiovisual and olfactory smorgasbord. The legacy of the Portuguese, who arrived in 1500, lives on in countless Baroque churches and in red-roofed houses with faded blue and white tile facades. But the aura of the streets let me and my companions know that we couldn't possibly be in Europe.

Samba blared from radios in tiny bars and crowded restaurants. Saleswomen wearing African-style head-ties and frilly white dresses called to us to browse in shops packed with handmade lace, jewelry and hammocks. Turbaned women were huddled over portable kitchens on street corners. When I stopped to investigate the source of the pungent aroma, I learned that the vendors were selling acarajé, known as acará in Nigeria, Benin and Togo. Made from mashed beans and dried shrimp, these delicious fritters were spread with a sauce of onions, peppers and ginger. Vats of bubbling rust-colored dendê (palm oil—common in both Bahian and African cooking) were used for frying.

Pedestrians gathered in plazas to watch men perfect their skills at capoeira, a martial art from Angola. Forbidden to fight, slaves disguised this form of self-defense as dance. Two crouching men would face each other, gesturing fluidly as if on the verge of coming to blows. Then with lightning-speed kicks, spins and flips, each would just miss connecting with the other's flashing limbs. Musicians quickened the pace as they played drums and plucked the berimbau, made from a taut cord attached to a tall curved stick and a gourd. Suddenly I was on a Manhattan street corner watching a group of kids break dance.

While most Bahians are devout Catholics, many also practice the mystical Candomblé religion of Nigeria's Yorubas. Ironically, the Catholic Church played a major (though unintentional) role in insuring that many African beliefs and customs were never lost. Slaves simply camouflaged their banned religions. They pretended to worship Catholic saints who had traits that paralleled those of their orixás (gods). Each orixá represents a natural or spiritual force.

We spent an evening as the only outsiders at one of Bahia's frequent Candomblé ceremonies. In the middle of a room overflowing with neighborhood residents, participants danced to pounding drums. Although most Bahians have never been to Africa, the musicians were singing in Yoruba—the old Yoruba that hasn't been spoken in Nigeria for generations. Apparently possessed by orixás, dancers would suddenly fall to the floor in a wild, euphoric, trance-like state. The ekedi, women who assisted the participants, would lead them into another room to be calmed and then dressed in the colorful, flowing costumes of the gods who had found their way into the dancers' bodies.

I remembered the first time I saw a woman "get the spirit" in a black American Baptist church. Just like the ekedi, the women around her had tenderly wiped the perspiration from her face after she jolted, trembling and thrashing, out of her seat.

Another night we attended a party in the courtyard of an old fort. Their hands flying up and down on drums that stood in neat rows, members of one of the city's

Bloco Afros [Afro-Brazilian carnival clubs] set many hips in motion. During carnival, these associations come out in full force. In preparation for the annual festivities, members study Bantu, Yoruba or another African culture to be incorporated into their music, songs and dance.

As we shook a leg or two, I looked around at the many heads of hair in all its natural splendor—thick braids, thin cornrows, dense curls, waistlong dreadlocks. This outward display of black pride hadn't always been so common in Bahia. Brazilian slaves and their descendants may never have relinquished their religions, music, dance, food and portions of their language. But like black Americans, Afro-Brazilians had been led to believe that beauty should be measured by European standards, that the straighter the hair and the lighter the skin, the better.

Unfortunately, many Brazilians (and Americans, despite our awakening during the 60s and 70s) still cling to this misguided notion. The existence of mulattoes (people of both African and European descent) is often cited to "prove" the "absence" of race-related problems. Yet inherent in the term itself is the belief that Afro-Brazilians with European blood are more attractive, desirable and somehow better human beings than their darker cousins. Still, mulattoes are hardly immune from discrimination at the hands of Brazilian whites. Mulatto women, often viewed as exotic sex objects, are treated with a combination of reverence and condescension. The welcome profusion of natural hair styles we saw in Bahia was one indication of the healthier consciousness that has begun to sprout. This trend made it easier for me to cope with the country's socio-political ills, including its pervasive poverty.

My mother tells a story of an encounter with a porter at a game reserve lodge in Kenya, during her first trip to Africa. The man wondered what part of America she was from. She told him New York, and, recognizing the large holes in his earlobes, asked if he was Masai. Nodding proudly, he inquired, "And what is your tribe?" When my mother answered him with a blank stare, he exclaimed, disbelief and pity pinching his brow, "You mean you don't know?"

While, in a sense, Brazil's vibrant culture had sent me on my first trip to Africa, I did not come any closer to knowing the countries, languages or tribes of my forebears. But poking around Bahia did give me a glimpse, in vivid Technicolor, of how my past had shaped me.